"In a sea of Instagrammy witchy content, *Spells for the Apocalypse* . . . delivers much-needed education, nervous system tending, and a dose of re-enchantment. And the footnotes are an added bonus!" —BECCA PIASTRELLI, author of *Root and Ritual*

"This compelling book is a potent reminder that we are active characters in our personal and collective lives, that each one of us can affect change through intention, will, and action." —MARIA MINNIS, author of *Tarot for the Hard Work*

"This book is essential for the modern witch's library, for anyone who wants to hold themselves and their people tenderly without turning their back to the storm."
    —DANIELLE DULSKY, author of *The Holy Wild*

"With warmth and wisdom, Carmen Spagnola shares simple yet potent rituals and remedies to help you find your footing, create meaning, and nurture hope as you confront the challenges of our rapidly changing world."
    —MARA GLATZEL, author of *Needy: How to Advocate for Your Needs and Claim Your Sovereignty*

T0283762

SPELLS

for the

APOCALYPSE

ALSO BY CARMEN SPAGNOLA

The Spirited Kitchen:
Recipes and Rituals for the Wheel of the Year

SPELLS
for the
APOCALYPSE

PRACTICAL
MAGIC FOR
TURBULENT
TIMES

Carmen Spagnola

Countryman Press
An Imprint of W. W. Norton & Company
Independent Publishers Since 1923

This book is a general information resource for people who want to try self-help magical practices. It is not a substitute for medical or psychological diagnosis, treatment, or therapeutic support. The author is not a psychologist, psychiatrist, psychotherapist, or other board-certified mental health professional. Please be sure to note the places in the book where the author advises the reader to consult a mental health professional, and definitely do so if you enact any ritual in this book and you feel worse afterward. If you are experiencing a mental health or physical emergency, please go to your nearest emergency room. If you have a severe mood or personality disorder, or if you suffer from suicidality, traumatic brain injury, or psychosis, even though some of the rituals in this book may be helpful to you, advice for managing those conditions is completely beyond the scope of this book. Please, also, consult your healthcare provider before attempting some of the physical activities described in this book, including, without limitation, activity outdoors, immersion in cold water, or lifting heavy objects. Any URLs displayed in this book link or refer to websites that existed as of press time. The publisher is not responsible for, and should not be deemed to endorse or recommend, any website other than its own or any content that it did not create. The author, likewise, is not responsible for any third-party material.

For information about permission to reproduce selections from this book, write to Permissions, Countryman Press, 500 Fifth Avenue, New York, NY 10110

For information about special discounts for bulk purchases, please contact W. W. Norton Special Sales at specialsales@wwnorton.com or 800-233-4830

Manufacturing by Versa Press
Book design by Beth Steidle
Production manager: Devon Zahn

Countryman Press
www.countrymanpress.com

An imprint of W. W. Norton & Company, Inc.
500 Fifth Avenue, New York, NY 10110
www.wwnorton.com

978-1-68268-951-6

10 9 8 7 6 5 4 3 2 1

To all the Numini

CONTENTS

Introduction • ix

PART I
Part Magic, Part Self-Help • 1

PART II
Rituals • 39

PART III
Remedies • 121

Acknowledgments • 195

Index • 197

Now Is a Moment of Great Need

✦ ✦ ✦ ✦ ✦

What you hold in your hands, dear reader, is a handbook for turbulent times.

Apocalypse is a somewhat dramatic word to describe collapse.[1] It sounds almost mythical, but it's actually a rather mundane experience of ever-eroding infrastructure, ideology, social fabric, and ecosystems. Things limp along for quite a while before they are suddenly, and sometimes shockingly, rendered nonfunctional. Collapse is like descending a staircase and missing the last few steps. It happens slowly and then all of a sudden. You find yourself in a heap, shaken and disoriented, and likely in a lot of pain. You knew you were going down but didn't expect to land quite so hard.

Collapse can be experienced personally or collectively. We have a personal experience of collapse when a beloved dies, or when we go through a breakup, suffer sudden illness or chronic disability, or experience job loss. Collective collapse is about living through the converging emergencies of large-scale cooperation dilemmas for which there are no timely solutions. These large-scale predicaments include climate chaos, the dissolution of empire states, pandemics, and the widespread failures of capitalism. Turbulent times, indeed!

Collapse, whether personal or collective, induces a nervous system response called the freeze state. It happens when our nervous system gets so overwhelmed that our body and mind grind to a halt. Freeze impacts us on the physical, emotional, mental, and even spiritual level. You might experience bone-deep fatigue with little or no physical exertion, stiffness and heaviness in your limbs, a slow heart rate, shallow breathing, even slight numbness in your face or extremities. You may have a flat affect, monotone voice, still face, or feel devoid of emotion. You may feel mentally checked out, foggy, or nonverbal, and you may lack focus, procrastinate, be unable to read, and have low motivation. Spiritual malaise can ensue with chronic feelings of dread or aimlessness, questioning your life's meaning and purpose.[2]

Just a little further along in this book, we'll talk about different forms of freeze and how you can use the Rituals and Remedies within these pages to gently come out of freeze into relative safeness, and mobilize enough to take the next small step on your healing journey.

Bless This Mess

If you've picked up this book, probably on some level you are not doing okay. And that's okay! As you use this book as a tool for healing and a way to process traumatic experiences, you might feel confronted with complex, mixed-up feelings. They are all welcome. Especially if you feel responsible, even unintentionally, for a terrible outcome, or for hurting someone, or for scarring the planet. You are worthy of spiritual care, even for that. In our Rituals, let's make space for deep acknowledgment of how we're impacted by painful experiences, and also for reckoning with the marks we've left on others and the imprints in our wake. We may not be our best self while we're struggling. Humans hurt and get hurt. There's no way to completely avoid that.

In your lifetime, you'll have both victim and perpetrator experiences. Ancestrally, you may have both oppressor and oppressed lineages. Ritual helps hold your experiences, with nuance. Late-stage racialized capitalism is not exactly the golden age of nuance, but do your best to hold multiple truths. You might feel like shit right now, yes. *And,* it probably won't always be this way. You want to escape feeling guilt or shame or grief, *and* you also want to face life head-on and own what's yours to carry. You're tired and you just want to go home, *and also,* this is it. This is home. It's a but/and/both situation.

Using the practices in this book, we're cultivating capacity for nuance and paradox. Aim to bring some consciousness to what you consider sacred and what feels unworthy. In other words, interrogate which parts of yourself you want to heal, which parts you don't really want to look at, which parts you want to hide or ignore, and why. It makes sense to be scared of sitting with the hard stuff. I deeply understand not wanting to open a can of worms we can't contain. What if we start looking into all the sludgy, hard feelings, and we wind up discovering that we are somehow just . . . bad? What if we feel like we kind of deserve to feel like crap?

Wow. Things can go south real quick, can't they? That's what trauma brain will do—it will have you jumping to the worst possible conclusion, spiraling and catastrophizing before you can even say, "I am not worthy of love."

You are inherently worthy of love. This is true even if you somehow contributed to painful experiences, your own or someone else's. I bet we can point to somewhere along the line where you were utterly failed by the world around you. You deserve to be witnessed in that. Your pain matters. With the help of this book, we can hold the complexity of whatever you're going through.

We can also support you in letting go of any preoccupation you might have with how you'd like to be perceived, and instead deal with how you really are and what you're really feeling. Your truth matters. Whether you want to deal with your true feelings or not, they are there, ever-present, persistent, and needing to be dealt with, like the microplastics of the psychospiritual world.

Through this book, we'll work to lift the taboo and stigma from experiencing ugly, difficult feelings. In the same way, we'll also be inclusive with our materia magica and what we deem "spiritual." Magic doesn't have to be pretty. You do not need to have an altar that is Instagrammy. You don't need to purchase sleek supplies from an occult shop. You don't need to look trendy, "witchy," or youthful. You don't need to own a brown wide brim hat or decorate your sacred space in a particular style, be it Beige Mom or something from a Nancy Meyers movie. Let's uncouple our spiritual practice from capitalism. *Huzzah!* If we're really going to do the work of diving into the shadows, let's begin with ditching the need for our practice to have a fetching aesthetic. Let's aim to arrive at a place where all the messy parts are included as a beautiful byproduct of the disaster of our times.

Why Ritual in Turbulent Times?

✦ ✦ ✦ ✦ ✦

For about two years in my marriage, I was dangling at the end of my rope. All the couples therapy, individual counseling, Non-Violent Communication workshops, somatic attunement exercises, attachment theory, and interpersonal neurobiology stuff was just . . . not working. We had opposing desires, exhausting careers, and limited energy in reserve for old wounds that stubbornly refused to heal. In exasperation, my husband implored, *Is there some kind of ritual you want us to do to help us, like . . . fix this?*

And so began our co-creation of the Ritual of the Marriage Moon. Each full moon from 2019 through 2020, we opened a bottle of cheap bubbly wine and sat down at our dining table with a large scroll of paper and drew two columns on it. The columns were titled, Carmen's Needs | Ruben's Needs. We each wrote down all the needs we had that were not currently being met by each other. We also had a diagram depicting us in the middle and our priorities radiating outward, like this:

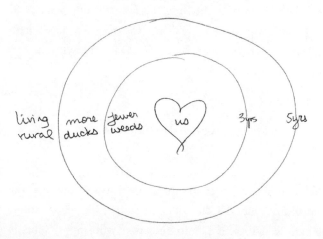

We each would read our list of needs while the other simply listened without argument. At the end of our list, we read out a declaration:

This is important to me, and I trust that when you have the capacity, you'll meet these needs.

For now, I give them to the Moon.

In essence, we made a deal with each other every month. We'd each work to trust that the other wanted to meet our needs, even if they couldn't right now. They would if they could, but they can't. It was a "can't do" problem, not a "doesn't want to do" problem. We also had to listen to each other's needs without arguing over them. We didn't judge, defend, negotiate, none of that. We just listened respectfully. We did this over and over, for almost two years.

At the end of each ritual, we lit a fire, tossed in a few branches of rosemary, and cleansed ourselves in the smoke, then poured an offering of extra proof alcohol over the flames saying, *And so it is.*

One time, right after I poured the offering and the flames leapt high into the sky, an owl alighted upon the fence post, not 10 feet away. It was such novel behavior—it definitely felt like a sign that the Greater Powers were listening. Like they wanted us to know they'd take care of us. *Message received!*

As time passed, we each worked to prioritize the needs on each other's lists. Ruben picked up more of the mental load of the household by learning to cook new recipes and taking over assigned dinner-making nights. We settled on a regular housekeeping rhythm, which was high on Ruben's list of needs.

Eventually, we arrived under the full moon and discovered that trust was there. The ritual had transformed us. The moon blessed us and carried us through a turbulent time in our marriage. The owl has been our protector ever since. With openness and creativity, we made space for a new form of outside help and it worked. Now we have a stronger relationship not only with each other but also with the Greater Benevolent Powers that envelope us in their care. We haven't done this ritual for a long time now but it's in our toolkit if we need it, and surely, given the times we find ourselves in, we'll need it again someday.

Ritual is what you do when you want to see a change in your life. Ritual couples action with will, and summons the Greater Benevolent Powers to assist. All spells are rituals. They're an active declaration of a desire for something to be different. We're casting spells all the time, consciously or unconsciously, with our thoughts, words, and deeds. Affirmations are spells. Self-talk is spellcraft. Journaling is spell-ing.

The difference between a spell and a ritual is merely a matter of degree. The effect of a simple spell might last an hour, a day, or a week, whereas a ritual that is well considered and involves some amount of inner and outer preparation can have very long-lasting effects. Sense what happens in your body when you consider the difference: A spell is like asking the Universe out on a date; a ritual is like getting engaged. Can you feel the difference? Ritual has some heft. It helps bring equilibrium to our spiritual life; we meet and match the moment of need with an appropriate level of attention, time, and attunement.

How to Use This Book

This is a handbook for an embodied and emotionally attuned spiritual practice. It's easy to use: You feel a certain way, you do something about it. Simply open to the contents pages of Rituals (page 39) or Remedies (page 121), identify the chapter that best fits your feelings, and follow the instructions.

But while this book is easy to use, I really don't think you should read it as you would a normal book, front to back. That would be too much of a major bummer. This is more like a *Choose Your Own Adventure* book. If you try to read it cover to cover, you're likely to get stuck and not make it to the triumphant end of the adventure. Part II contains all the calamities (and attendant rituals) in alphabetical order, and Part III consists of Remedies. The Remedies appear at the end of the book to anchor the material, just like we might end a therapy session—with grounding, safeness, and stability.

In order to avoid getting bogged down in Part II, you'll want to read the Rituals selectively as needed. In fact, feel free to begin with Part III. Start practicing the Remedies today! If you're a type A personality who just can't do that, and you *really* can't wait to read all the Rituals, I beg of you: titrate between the Rituals and the Remedies.

Do read the Author's Notes—this is really important! They are a sanctuary of sober second thought, and the act of flipping to them will literally slow your roll. They provide context and offer a tangible speed bump to ensure you're proceeding at a trauma-sensitive pace. They'll help you decide if it's the right Ritual or Remedy for you at this time.[3]

Always end your reading session with a Remedy. The Remedies will equip you with skills for living thoughtfully, beautifully, present, and connected, even in the most turbulent times.

Author's Notes
....

1 For a primer on collapse: Spagnola, Carmen. "Collapse in a Nutshell." The Numinous Podcast, episode 161. March 22, 2022. https://crspagnola.podbean.com/e/tnp161-collapse-in-a-nutshell-with-carmen-spagnola/.

2 Because the freeze state looks rather docile from the outside and can feel somewhat numb on the inside, it's easy to downplay the seriousness of it. In fact, the freeze state indicates that we're at the highest

level of distress. When we're stressed, we go into fight, flight, fidget, or fawn states. Beyond that, a perceived life threat thrusts our nervous system into the freeze state.

3   Thank you for reading the Author's Notes! Max Liboiron wrote the most entertaining and spiritually satisfying book on plastics and pollution that you'll ever read. It inspired my decision to use notes in this book. These notes are a way for us to draw a little closer so I can share background and context without distracting from the main text. It's also where I'll point you to incredible teachers and resources, cite my learning lineage, and sometimes make a joke. These notes are also a way to resist extractive reading, which can lead to spiritual appropriation and commodification—we create additional space here to hold complexity and open doors to new ways of thinking and being together. It's part of being relational and real with you as a fellow journeyer through collapse times. Learning to survive terrible things requires a synthesis of highly personal influences and unique processes of experience and integration. This book is a helpful framework, but there are webs upon webs of knowledge that have shaped it. You might need to follow some of the threads in the endnotes to come up with your own personal methodology.

I highly recommend you read *Pollution Is Colonialism* even just for the footnotes alone. It's like getting two books in one! Thank you Alysha Seriani for introducing me to Liboiron's work.

Liboiron, Max. *Pollution Is Colonialism*. Duke University Press, 2021.

PART I

*Part Magic,
Part Self-Help*

Trauma-Informed Witchcraft

✦ ✦ ✦ ✦ ✦

The spells in this book are grounded in principles that align with trauma recovery because living through apocalypse is inherently traumatizing. This can be deeply challenging material to deal with, even in therapy. What's more, few people can find professional therapeutic support that's a good fit, much less afford it on an ongoing basis. In the age of the Long Emergency, I believe we'll need to make do and muddle through, attending to our own and each other's mental wellness needs in a more community-based way. In collapse, we are all "barefoot doctors" on the frontlines of trauma.[1] But if you heed my advice, drawn from experts, research scientists, and trauma recovery educators of our time, you'll gain a ton of insight, skill, and resourcing to carry you through your life in a more future-proofed way.

That's not to say that you can't still possibly get hurt. It's painful work at times to face stark realities and admit how much we're struggling. Plus, a lot of us are good at hurting ourselves by pushing through signs of distress, desperately doing too much, and ignoring our body's "no" signals, because we want so badly to be healed and feel better. (It's me, hi, I'm the problem.)

Let's outline a few helpful reminders so we stay in bounds, within our zone of tolerance, and ensure we are responsible for ourselves and our magic.

GROUNDING: Don't do spellcraft while you're in a tizzy. Your magic will be chaotic and the results may disappoint. Always begin by grounding yourself. Close your eyes or look at the ground, take some natural breaths, wait for things to change in your body toward a calmer, more settled state before you begin.

SAFETY FIRST: We always dose the field with safeness before we do any healing work. That can mean orienting to what's comforting in the room, finding the place in the body that feels the most resourced, or calling in spiritual allies for protection, encouragement, and strength. Anytime we get stuck or feel overwhelmed in a practice, we pause to dose the field with more safeness again before proceeding.

CONSENT, CHOICE, AND AGENCY: I encourage you to tailor your spellcraft to your unique needs. There's no need for dogmatic adherence to the specific instructions as written. This is not a religion. You do not need to perform the role of "good student." You can modify or opt out of any part. As long as it's within your comfort zone and you're not becoming flooded with emotion or sensation, take risks with your self-expression and celebrate yourself for doing so!

TRANSPARENCY: Please read the Author's Notes for important context and attribution. They will lead you to an even deeper well of resources and excellent teachers to expand your practice. Citation and proper credit to teachers is part of anticolonial practice.

HUMILITY: Honor the Spirits of Place by naming whose land you're on before you begin your magic. Be honest with yourself about the legacy of your ancestors. Honor your ancestors and heal the trauma of violation by pivoting patterns of harm including spiritual theft, erasure, and exploitation. Draw practices and inspiration from your own heritage. In the rich tapestry of human spirituality, there is no need for appropriation. Name the teachers in your lineage and credit their work if you're leading or sharing publicly.

SLOWER IS BETTER, AND LESS IS MORE: If you're getting a "healing hangover"—feeling foggy brained, sluggish, headachy, or ruminating, you might have overdone it and spent a bit too long or gone a bit too deep into a practice. Incremental work and bite-size amounts are best. If you go too fast or do too much, you can do more harm than good. It's amazing how so little attention can produce so much effect.

AFTERCARE: We owe a duty of care to ourselves, not just to make time for our spiritual life, but to track the impacts of our healing work and make sure we're doing okay afterward. We can't just turn our feelings on and off, and sometimes these practices have a delayed effect. In the hours and days after a Ritual or Remedy, please return often to the basics of self-care. Remember to H.A.L.T.: Are you hungry, angry, lonely, or tired? Stop for a moment and tend to your need before you proceed.

SUPPORT, COMMUNITY, AND MUTUAL SELF-HELP: Humans cannot heal in isolation. We require witnessing, validation, and a sense of "getting gotten" in order to satisfy our biological need for reassurance that we can survive here. Especially in turbulent times, we need the added support of a therapist, a community of practice, and/or at least one friend.[2] They can be online or in-person, one-on-one or in a group setting, and you can be actively or passively engaged, but you've gotta go get some support, my friend. A book is a great start to help you become aware of what might be missing in your toolkit and how you can fill the gaps, but, ultimately, our sense of security and healing come from interpersonal neurobiology—two or more nervous systems signaling back and forth that we've got each other and we're gonna be okay.

Ritual as Both Mobilization and Containment

✦ ✦ ✦ ✦ ✦

Ritual is a deliberate activity that supports us when emerging from freeze, as described in the introduction. In order to stay current with our everyday stress management and to recover from significant losses or traumatic experiences, intense emotions require both containment and release. Ritual provides exactly that. Spells help us discharge stress, stabilize and resource ourselves, ground ourselves in the present moment, and restore our nervous system through co-regulation with the More Than Human.

A good ritual is a sturdy container. It's well sealed with no energetic leaks or distractions. With a clear beginning, middle, and end, we can sense the boundary of it. It's a well-defined world unto itself where we enact a scene from our life's drama. Ritual is a liminal space we occupy to regroup, recover our instincts, focus attention, process feelings, gain strength and clarity, and transform the nebulous into something tactile and comprehensible.

Ritual is an intermediary realm with the ordinary world on one side of the threshold and the non-ordinary world of Spirit on the other. When we enact a ritual, we're showing the Greater Powers the change we'd like to see in our lives so they can fill in the gaps like a paint-by-numbers.

You know when your hands are so cold they sting? If you run your freezing cold hands under cold water, it actually feels warm. Recall that achy pins-and-needles feeling as your fingers begin to thaw. It's an uncomfortable process, right? Coming out of a freeze state is similar: rapid embodiment can suddenly flood us with a lot of uncomfortable feelings. Our body might blow a circuit—*Too much, too fast, too soon!*

When we become flooded, our nervous system will move us to dissociate in order to protect us from all that

TYPES OF FREEZE

Attentive immobility: You're like a deer in headlights, hyperaware of your surroundings but unable to act.

Tonic immobility: Your body goes rigid. Your brain goes offline. You are human camouflage.

Collapsed immobility: You feel like a dead fish or possum, floppy, sleepy, and unresponsive.

Functional freeze: You're tasking, buzzing around like a busy bee, yet feel disconnected, out of touch, functioning on autopilot, and life is a blur.

pain and distress. Dissociation is a sense of disconnection from your senses, thoughts, sense of self, or personal history. Some people feel a sort of "unreality" and lose contact with time, place, and identity.

Dissociation gets a bad rap because to others we can seem inattentive, disengaged, dismissive, or uncaring. In fact, we are *so* impacted by what's happened or been said that our body has pressed pause and is no longer able to function according to typical social mores. Dissociation is an amoral condition; it is not bad, it is not good, it is simply a state signaling that we have become overwhelmed. Though it may be frustrating or happen at inopportune times, dissociation is a merciful and useful evolutionary impulse.

Freeze and its cousin, dissociation, are not all bad. Sometimes, they're downright great! They endeavor to keep us safe and shield us from threats. They perform a protective function. There's no need to eliminate them from our toolkit of coping strategies. It's only when freeze prevents us from achieving desired outcomes that this otherwise totally logical and reasonable response becomes a problem.

A better way to shift out of dissociation and emerge from freeze is through incremental mobilization. You really don't want to come out of freeze too quickly. It's best to gently mobilize with small movements, gentle activities, lots of self-attunement, and care. Slowly, slowly, we discharge the stress that put us into freeze in the first place.

QUALITIES OF DISSOCIATION

Daydreaming: Your mind can't stay focused and instead drifts off, lost in thought or fantasy.

Memory loss: You zone out and lose time, or certain events, people, information, or time periods just don't seem to stick in your brain.

Distortion: A blurred sense of reality that seems very out of step with other people's perspectives or consensus reality.

Disconnection: Feeling detached from people, emotions, things you love, and distant from your surroundings.

Psychic numbness: Feeling indifferent, shut down, lacking empathy.

Altered time: Difficulty tracking time, or feeling like you're timeline shifting, constantly cycling through past and future but straining to arrive in the present. Flashbacks can trigger a sense of lost time or blackout.

Derealization: For some, the world seems uncanny or unreal, like looking through a warped window pane or as though they're living in a movie.

We also want to consider what you're moving *into* when you come out of freeze.

If you've gone into freeze because the environment is overwhelming, it's not that helpful to emerge from freeze directly into that same context. It's exhausting and repetitive, and you run the risk of being retraumatized.

Ideally, you instead emerge into an environment that is safe enough and soothing enough to find your footing a bit before you face the overwhelming world. That's why so many trauma therapists insist on establishing a "safe place" in one's imagination before doing any deep work, and cocreate aftercare plans with their clients toward the end of a session.

Throughout this book, but especially in Part II, you'll find we do a lot of scanning for safeness, working with comforting allies, grounding before we cast our spells, pausing, pacing, self-attuning, and ending the rituals with a strong sense of closure and stability. These principles continue in the Remedies in Part III, which are entirely about creating a robust sense of safeness, support, resourcefulness, and belonging in your life.

Dosing the Field with Safeness

The Rituals will not always feel awesome. Not at first. I'm sorry to say that sitting with our Anxiety, Dread, Fear,

Grief, or Overwhelm is no fun, no matter how we try to dress them up. There's no safe haven from the complexities of interlocking systems of oppression, or from intersecting identities and social location, or from change, contradiction, or paradox. Reality bites and there are no truly "safe spaces" in apocalypse times.

In light of reality, "safe enough" is the more achievable metric.

We can, and I believe we should, strive for brave spaces that help us to grow and rise to a challenge, which necessarily means we'll be a bit uncomfortable some of the time.[3]

We're going to craft rituals that feel safe enough to participate in, yet are challenging enough to transform us. That's the purpose of ritual, after all: to inspire change.

While many folks are not consciously aware how much trauma is carried in their body, others are acutely aware.[4] Given that *the horrors never cease,* as the kids say, in trauma-sensitive witchcraft we eschew the idea of a perfect sense of safety and instead reach for layers of safe*ness.*

To craft the ritual container, we'll regularly "dose the field" with safeness.[5] We'll keep adding more and more layers of safeness—"this feels safer than that"—until we land on a combination of elements that feels safe *enough.* We're aiming for a process that feels safe enough to proceed and solid enough to hold you. You can stop at any time, make any adjustment necessary, and go at the pace that's right for you.

Apocalypse is exhausting. As we've already learned, the freeze response goes hand in hand with collapse. Just the thought of a ritual might seem like too much effort. That's normal and totally okay! Thanks to the miracle of neuroplasticity, even just thinking about a ritual can have major benefits and be surprisingly effective.

It's a bit like dreaming: Your heart rate, breathing, and sometimes even your muscles respond to your dream. Similarly, your brain can't necessarily tell the difference between you physically enacting a ritual versus performing it on the mental level.[6] When it comes to magic and spellcraft, "fantasy" is as potent as "reality," it just plays out in other dimensions. I still consider it full participation if you close your eyes, imagine the ritual unfolding, attune to sensations and emotions as you go along, and take steps toward aftercare as needed when you're done.

The Elements of Ritual

Turbulent times have a momentum to them. Change begets change. Things that seemed immutable, unalterable, like capital "T" Truth, are more susceptible to change as they get caught up in the spirit of the moment. It's disorienting—it seems nothing is safe from a tidal wave of upheaval. There's no denying it's painful, yet with open-mindedness and creativity, moments of great change can help us overcome inertia, spur innovation, and make space for new ideas and contributions.

A spell is a spiritual action to intentionally create change in your life. What makes it spiritual is that you enlist the help of other-than-human allies, including the Elements, to bring about this change. Elements carry energies, associations, and symbolic meaning. They can be a stand-in for a sentiment or intention. They can symbolize a physical, emotional, or mental state. They convey and amplify messages and add a certain emphasis or inflection to your magic. They bring a vibe.

Western occult traditions work with the Four Classical Elements: Earth, Air, Fire, and Water. The wuxing tradition (known in English as the Chinese Five Element philosophy), which appears in Traditional Chinese Medicine, astrology, feng shui, and metaphysics, works with Wood, Fire, Earth, Metal, and Water. Ayurveda employs Air, Fire, Water, Earth, and Aether (Spirit), as does the Wiccan religion.[7] When we add candles to a birthday cake, we invoke the element of Fire and all it symbolizes—the divine spark, a creative life force energy, Spirit suddenly called into being. When we make a wish and blow out the candles, we are invoking the element of Air as we think good thoughts and use our breath to direct those thoughts into the ether, and the smoke carries those wishes on the wind to the helping spirits in the celestial realms. Include one or more Elements in your magic to augment its power.

As times change, our values change. Our needs change, so our Rituals change. Perhaps it's time we reconsider the Elements in the context of collapse, ongoing crisis, and resource constraints? Are there more Elements we want to include as fundaments of our modern practice?

The following are the Elements I consider the foundations of my modern spellcraft. Our ancestors were much more embedded in their ecosystems than most folks today. Living under capitalist-imperialist-white-supremacist-hetero-patriarchy, we have to work harder to root ourselves in the larger story of the Earth and reinforce our bond with the Other Than Humans. When crafting your rituals, I encourage you to experiment with combinations of the eight Elements offered here. Some are familiar and some are new categories that I feel ought to be elevated to reflect their importance in the world, certainly of today, especially of tomorrow.

Earth

When we need support, grounding, or a place to pause and rest, we call upon the Earth. The Earth element includes land, plants, and animals. Of course, there are the large or charismatic beings that readily capture our imagination such as Bears, Mountains, and Roses.[8] Yet part of our anticolonial approach to spellcraft is becoming more consciously aware of the invisible networks that support us. When we invoke the Earth element, we animate the entire web of life to infuse our magic.

This element includes all constituents of soil life—minerals, microbes, and organic matter, as well as bacteria, protozoa, mites, nematodes, fungi, earthworms, ants, and insects. Some of these allies convey messages for us along hidden networks. Whenever I want to send a message to a certain sit spot on one of my favorite mountains far away, I place my hand on the trunk of the Ash tree in my backyard and ask them to pass it along for me. I envision the underground mycelial network lighting up as it carries my love across the land.

Within our own bodies, we remember our gut flora with its parasites and viruses, right down to the Demodex mites (those lil' guys that live in our eyebrows). These are all collaborators that make up the Earth element. Spiritual intimacy with these aspects of the Earth element can help us adopt a more accepting and respectful attitude toward the microorganisms that are our roommates and neighbors, to become more humble and studious learners of all they have to teach us. Our future as a species is more dependent on good relations with them than we, large and charismatic as we humans are, may care to admit.

Water

Around 400 million years ago, our aquatic ancestors emerged from the sea to become the origin point of our evolutionary lineage. As such, Water is the womb of the world. We call upon Water for nurturance, energetic cleansing, to process emotions, and find balance. This element helps us flow and function more rhythmically in life. To represent Water, we call upon the Moon, who rules the tides and embodies the changeable nature of water and life itself.

Water can be as comforting as a babbling brook or have the icy chill of snow. It can surprise us with its voluminous power and velocity. It can be calm and serene, or tumultuous and roiling. It can be refreshing and quenching, or brackish and fetid. Without motion, Water can quickly create a condition of squalor and stagnation. For this reason, it's important to consider the specific qualities of Water you want to invoke in your ritual. Consider the energetic difference between a clear glass bowl of fresh clean spring water, versus a black bowl of salt water, or an image of a waterfall in a rainbow mist. They each evoke something different, yes?

Water encompasses the world of dreams, the depths of our intuition, and an amniotic state of connection to the collective unconscious. Water can be represented by fluids, colors, seashells, aquatic animals, waterfowl, mirrors, and mermaids.

The Air teaches us to adjust our sails in the winds of fate. It rules over things that cannot be seen, only their influence felt. Air represents the realm of the mind and its creative potency. It represents the breath of Spirit, which conceives an idea before it is manifest. We invoke Air to support provocative thought, teaching and scholarship, clear communication, discernment, negotiation of the social contract, navigation of moral dilemma, insight, strategy, fairness, revolution, justice, and peace.

When Air wreaks havoc, life is chaotic and stormy. We can't fight the wind, so we must take shelter and wait for the storm to pass. We can do appeasement rituals while we're waiting. We can employ breath, sound, or smoke as a form of sympathetic magic to encourage the Air to behave mildly. We can burn incense, sing softly, chant or tone, play an instrument, or read aloud from a book of wisdom. If you feel stuck, listless, or mentally overwhelmed with life, invoke Air to shake things up. Open all the windows, hang a wind chime, look at the clouds, climb to a high peak in search of wind.

Symbols of Air include feathers and high-flying birds, clouds, thunder, outer space, temples and places of contemplation, and deities associated with the wind and weather such as Aura and Aeolus of Greek mythology, Thor from Scandinavia, Feng Popo (known as Madame Wind) in

China, Amun from Egypt, the loa Bade from Haiti, and Huracan, the Mayan god of wind. Research your heritage to discover how your wayback people related to wind and weather and how they named their gods. Research and study are forms of invocation to call in the power of Air.

Fire

The element of Fire teaches us about mutability, transformation, and the inner flame that we associate with the human spirit. It's so intimately connected with the nature of human existence that we use its connotations to describe the spark of divinity, flames of passion, embers of hope, and the light of consciousness. In many pagan traditions, Fire is considered the soul of the world, the inception point of all creation, as the Sun to the Earth.

When working with Fire, we're working with change. Octavia Butler laid it out for us in her book, *Parable of the Sower:*

> *All that you touch*
> *You Change.*
>
> *All that you Change*
> *Changes you.*

The only lasting truth
is Change.

God
is Change.[9]

We might treat Fire as divinity itself, just as the Roman goddess Vesta and the Greek Hestia before her are likely personifications that evolved from a time when Fire itself was worshipped as a god. Fire represents the realm of creativity, emerging spontaneously at times from seemingly nothing, able to alter everything it touches without itself ever able to be touched. Fire is a shape-shifter, catalyst, volatile, prone to taking large leaps, is neither solid nor liquid but can be present in both. We associate Fire with imagination, courage, boldness, charisma, energy, power, success, momentum, survival, speed, appetite, magic, vision, and conjuring that which cannot be perceived by the rational mind.

In turbulent times ahead, in this age of increasing wildfires that professor Stephen J. Pyne coined as "the pyrocene," we'll need to learn to live in a more attuned and responsive way with Fire. Many of us will have a closeness and familiarity with Fire that we did not and would not choose. How do we live with a devouring God? We accept Change. We try to shape Change. We prepare to survive Change. To rise from the ashes, the phoenix needs to burn.[10]

Metal

What are these times we live in if not a transformation by trial?[11] Metal is also an element of change, but it requires collaboration with Fire and other powerful forces, plus skill and intense effort, to receive its new form. It has endurance, lasting thousands of years in some cases. An important lesson from Metal for collapse times is that this element is closely linked to the cycle of birth, death, and rebirth. Once smelted it can be formed, melted again, and recycled. It is iterative. It has structure and strength but can become liquid to assume a new, more useful formation. It tells us that nothing need be wasted. Try again.

Metal is associated with innovation, tooling, craftsmanship, severance, conflict, war, wealth, and adornment. Sometimes lustrous, sometimes cold, sometimes conducive to electricity, it can be brute and it can be surgical. Literally a generalist and jack-of-all-trades, certainly a precious commodity and trade good in the apocalypse, metal is linked with the legendary cultures and ambitious leadership of the Scythians, the pharaohs, and the Vikings, and great monuments to human ingenuity such as the Eiffel Tower, the Statue of Liberty, and the Statue of Unity.[12]

Metal urges us to think big and think long. Be willing and adaptable. Metal is scarce, yes, but holds less value in its raw form; creativity is currency. Don't be afraid of hard work or tough blows. Metal reminds us of the transcendent function within each of us that knows the origin and the resolution to every problem we face, champions our efforts, and rewards us through tribute and legacy. The Metal element sends the message to the future, *I was here.*

Plastic

In the future, humans will be foraging for plastics the way we currently do for wild strawberries and mushrooms. In some parts of the world, this already happens. If you're a person of a certain age, you might already have a plastic bag full of plastic bags. Some particularly nice bags might even be high-graded to a second special spot in your house for the good plastic bags. I'm happy for those bags. They're going to live pretty much forever and they deserve a good home. Especially if you consider all that plastics do for us.

We now know that Plastic, made from crude oil, does not, in fact, come from dinosaurs. It actually comes from phytoplankton and zooplankton—marine plants and animals—that predate the dinosaurs. Plastic derives from life forms that are unimaginably ancient. In their book *Pollution Is Colonialism,* Michif-settler professor and plastics pollution researcher, Max Liboiron, writes that Indigenous concepts of Land are about "relations between the material aspects some people might think of as landscapes—water, soil, air, plants, stars—and histories, spirits, events, kinships, accountabilities, and other people that aren't human."[13]

In that spirit, plastics and dinosaurs share a lineage with us as Earthlings, Land-dwellers. The dinosaurs are our ancestors. They can teach us about things that leave a mark and never go away. About loss and preciousness and making something out of what's left after destruction. About losing control and creating monstrous problems. About carrying capacity. They can teach us about mistakes and shame. They can be our guides and allies on the journey through the dark times.

Consider pulling a piece of plastic out of your recycling or garbage bin and placing it on your altar. It could be as simple as a plastic bottle that's used as a vase for flowers, or as elaborate as a sculpture you made from bits and pieces. How does it feel to place trash on the altar? If you feel mildly embarrassed or repulsed, see if you can tolerate it just for a little while. This came from the Earth, just like you. It is your ancestor, many millennia down the line. What does it have to say about persistence, adaptability, unyielding consequences, and ingenuity? Maybe there's something made of plastic that you use every day that warrants special acknowledgment, something you'd miss desperately if it was gone. It could be a small piece of greenhouse plastic that you lay on the altar with a prayer that there's still some of this miracle product around in the future to help us grow our food in the midst of climate chaos. That would be a really beautiful way to honor and elevate this ancestor.

Like plastics, reality isn't going anywhere. Turbulent times are here and we just have to muddle through. But perhaps to this endeavor we can bring a sense of *amor fati*— love of one's fate—where we perceive everything in our lives, including the troubling, the painful, the existential, the difficult, and the not conventionally beautiful, if not as "good," then at least as worthy of our attention and care.

The Numinous

A signature of the Numinous is a sense of poignance. Poignance is my favorite dilemma. Poignance is like beauty and pain swirling together. In the words of the artist formerly known as John Cougar, it hurts so good.[14]

Mysterium tremendum et fascinans is a Latin phrase, one used in Rudolf Otto's work on the concept of the "numinous," that refers to a mysterious power and transcendent presence that is both awe-inspiring and a little terrifying. It's wondrous yet overwhelming. Intimate and infinite. We are rapt and dissociated. We're uneasy in its presence but can't tear ourselves away. Through an attachment theory lens, it's a bit disorganized, all this *push—pull, pick me up—put me down, I want to feel you—not that close*. Wrestling with yearning to know the unknowable and desire to touch the untouchable while terrified of knowing and fearful of its touch is part of the poignance of being human. Anything that helps us grapple with paradox is a good teacher in collapse times. The Numinous helps us be in the Now with Long Time as our measure.

Part of the perplexing nature of the Numinous is that it's ever-present everywhere but is imperceptible through rational human consciousness. It's beyond understanding but deeply felt and experienced. It's such a mindbender that it's tempting to think of the Numinous as being so immeasurably vast that it's hardly worth trying to understand, much less experience directly. But that's not the way I think of the Numinous.

I think of it more like gravity—I don't have to believe in it for it to work, don't have to expend effort to experience it, and need no more proof of it than my own earthbound existence. The Numinous is my constant companion, shaping my experience in miraculous ways every moment I'm alive, and I expect it will continue even after I die. I think of the Numinous as a wave of sound or light, pulsing rhythmically, beaming the eternal message: *You are not alone in all this.*

Though the Numinous and the Cosmos are distinct, they're intertwined concepts of primordial mystery that often evoke each other— it's natural to contemplate the nature of the Universe after an encounter with the Numinous, and vice versa. Symbols that denote transcendence and ever-presence are unique to each culture, but anything related to the miraculous, or outer space, an all-seeing eye, blinding light, the Cosmic Egg, the music of the spheres, or sublime beauty come as close as possible to capturing the essence of the Numinous.[15]

DNA

In the folklore of my Scottish Highlander ancestors, one would never, ever leave their DNA lying about for anyone to steal—not a used hairbrush, a nail clipping, or even an eyelash. The fear is that someone could steal it and curse you with it. Apologies to the Old Ones, mine and those of any tradition that keeps this custom, but the number of folks who know how to perform an effective curse these days are fairly few—I don't worry too much about it, myself. Bigger problems to worry about what with, you know, *everything happening.*

We can work with DNA as a primal offering; a way of saying to the Cosmos, *Here is Me. I present to you all that I am. I give myself to you.*

Leaving a single strand of hair, a kiss, or your fingerprint on the altar also says, *I am so small. You are great beyond measure. There's no offering I can make to equal your formidable power and limitless wisdom. The only thing of me that matches your boundlessness is my eternal love for you, carried in the tiny vessel of my Being. Take this little bit of me—my love is as immense as my offering is miniscule.*

Finally, it's cliché but it's true: We are made of star-stuff.[16] We are Elemental. Sometimes it's tempting in these dire days to internalize a certain misanthropic notion that humans deserve whatever comes to us. Human-caused climate chaos, violence, oppression, and social inequity give us ample reasons not only to despair but to despise.

But most humans for the most part are actually very good people. And all of us are born intrinsically lovable. While it may not be genetically encoded in us, love has biological underpinnings that are deeply entwined in our nature, all of which arose having traveled through time and space to fall upon the Earth and make itself at home. We belong here. We belong to this planet and to this moment. Place yourself on the altar as an offering to the Unfathomable Mystery, a promise that you will do your part as loving witness to whatever unfolds, compost in this graveyard of stars.

Remedies as Resources

The Remedies in Part III are ongoing practices that increase our resilience, like preventative medicine for personal collapse. They slow the onset of the freeze response and increase our stamina. Most important for collapsey times, the Remedies enhance our sense of self-efficacy—the confidence to know we can perform under pressure and rise to the moment.

The Remedies are opportunities to practice satisfiability and enoughness, two critical capacities for enduring turbulent times.[17] When the human-made world is meager and cruel, we have to work hard to find meaning and motivation to continue. Frankly, I don't want to just endure my life or survive an apocalypse, I want to seed a flourishing future for tomorrow's humans and plants and animal kin. In order for that to happen, I need to start cultivating the soil for that future today. I need to do my part to uplift and conserve the craft of a beautiful life. I have to acquire the skills of appreciation, awe, and wholeness so I can pass them on.

If I am not satisfiable, but instead ever grasping for something better and more perfect, nothing will ever be enough. If I do not have a felt sense of satiation, instead always hungering for more, then the flourishing future can never arrive. It will forever remain out of reach. Only when I can land within myself a sense of enoughness can I feel satisfaction. When I feel satisfaction, I'm able to rest for a time in a state of well-being that restores the body, mind, and spirit, and which, paradoxically, summons the will to go on.

I recommend you try all the Remedies you feel drawn to and incorporate a few into your daily life. As you integrate them, they become resources you can recruit in a crisis and even share with others. They'll help you become the person you want to be in turbulent times.

SOMATIC-SPEAK

The term *somatics* refers to embodiment practices that bring attention to the mind-body connection, the inner self, and attunement to the sensations and emotions we feel.

Resourcing: Establishing feelings of safeness in your body or identifying soothing allies in the environment that help calm and comfort, as well as engender courage, if necessary.

Titration: The process of experiencing just small portions of distress at a time so as not to become overwhelmed.

Pendulation: Shifting focus from stress to nonstress, between expansion and contraction, to become more fluid with your attention and your ability to self-regulate.

Dysregulation: A completely normal and natural experience of distress in the nervous system due to a perception of threat where it becomes difficult to calm yourself or manage emotions. Sometimes it's temporary and passes quickly. For some folks, it can be a constant background state that leads to behavioral problems.

Self-regulation: The ability to settle the nervous system enough to manage emotions, thoughts, and energy states.

Co-regulation: An interactive process where engagement with a supportive Other helps you to manage your state, calm and soothe your nervous system, and enable you to self-regulate.

Even if you don't particularly believe in the Greater Powers, the More Than Human, spellcraft, witchcraft, or any kind of helping spirits, this book offers an assortment of self-help exercises grounded in interpersonal neurobiology

POWER THREAT MEANING FRAMEWORK

The PTM framework provides a long overdue conceptual alternative to the diagnostic model of psychiatric health (as laid out in the American Psychological Association's Diagnostic and Statistical Manual of Psychiatric Disorders). The PTMF acknowledges systems of oppression as a root cause of psychological distress.

and trauma recovery.[18] It is informed by attachment theory and polyvagal theory, and guided by principles outlined by the British Psychological Society's Power Threat Meaning Framework (PTMF).[19]

Instead of focusing only on symptoms and sensitizing events, in this approach we ask:

- How does power operate in your life? (What happened to you?)

- What kind of threats does it pose? (How did it affect you?)
- What is the meaning of these situations and experiences to you? (What sense did you make of it?)
- What kinds of threat response are you using? (How did you survive?)

The healing process moves even deeper when we explore the next two questions:

- What access to power resources do you have? (What are your strengths?)
- How does this all fit together? (What is your story?)

Think of this book as a way to explore these questions with your body, heart, mind, and, if you're open to it, your spirit. Each Ritual and Remedy identifies impacts, inner and outer resources, and strengths, and is meant to help you craft new storylines on your journey through turbulent times.

If You're a Spiritual Adept

There are thirteen Rituals and thirteen Remedies in this book. To work through them over the course of a year, I recommend doing the Ritual chapters leading up to or on the Full Moon. Do the Remedy chapter anytime, but especially during the New Moon and First Quarter phases.

If you are an experienced ritual practitioner, you may want to consider an annual rhythm of matching certain rituals to your seasonal or animist practice. When I lead wilderness quests, we spend four preparatory days immersed in the study of the spiritual lessons of the seasons. Certain lessons correspond neatly to rites of passage for specific times of year. The seasons and their rituals somewhat match the human journey from infancy to elderhood.

Everyone will have their own seasonal rhythm—if you're afflicted by seasonal affective disorder, you know this very well. To match a ritual to a season of life, ask yourself, *What are the key spiritual developmental tasks of spring, summer, fall, and winter?*

Here's how I would match the activities of this book to the seasons:

SPRING
Anxiety, Predicament, Dread, Awe, Renewal

SUMMER
Overwhelm, Rage, Celebration, Movement, Pronking

FALL
Confusion, Despair, Fear, Loss, Stagnation,
Acknowledgment, Balance, Connection, Conservation

WINTER
Burnout, Disquiet, Grief, Appreciation, Conservation, Nurturance, Protection

As you organize a year of your spiritual life around these spells, you'll find some rituals are worth doing many times. They'll become pillars of your holistic spiritual practice to revisit annually or for major life transitions.[20]

Author's Notes

1   The "barefoot doctors" was a program that ran in rural China from the 1930s through the 1980s. Doctors who had trained in Western schools didn't want to leave the urban centers and go back to their home villages. In response, the government implemented a six-month training program for farmers and rural residents to learn how to treat most medical needs outside of surgery and complex health conditions. Over one million people were trained as barefoot doctors, working 50 percent of the time on their farm and 50 percent of their time in their community. They focused on epidemic disease prevention, provided immunizations, and cured simple ailments using scientific techniques and medicines. If we think of ourselves as barefoot doctors on the frontlines of trauma, we will be better prepared in our homes and communities to meet the needs of the current mental health crisis.

Lee, Y., and Kim, H. "The Turning Point of China's Rural Public Health during the Cultural Revolution Period: Barefoot Doctors: A Narrative." *Iranian Journal of Public Health*, 47, Suppl 1, (2018): 1–8. PMID: 30186806; PMCID: PMC6124148.

"Barefoot doctors." Wikipedia. Accessed February 25, 2024. https://en.wikipedia.org/wiki/Barefoot_doctor.

2   Recommended resources for trauma-informed, intersectional, feminist witchcraft and ritual arts, quite easily found with a search of

Google or Instagram, include: Thérèse Cator (Embodied Black Girl), Taraneh Erfan (Mind on Spirit), Juliet Diaz (*Witchery*), Mimi Young (Ceremonie), Nikiah Seeds (Sacred Path School), Asha Frost (*You Are the Medicine*), Dayna Lynn Nuckoll (The People's Oracle), Cyndi Brannen (*Keeping Her Keys*), Sarah Faith Gottesdiener (*The Moon Book*), Toi Smith (Spell of Capitalism), Jen Lemen (Path of Devotion), Sarah Corbett (Rowan and Sage), Laura Tempest Zakroff (*Sigil Witchery*), Fanny Priest (The Trauma Witch), Pam Grossman (*Waking the Witch*), and my membership site, The Numinous Network, to name a few.

3   Thank you, Desiree Adaway, for the language and practice of "brave space."

4   Sometimes we're so acutely aware of sensation in the body that the novelty of safeness itself triggers a trauma response. For more on this see Kain, Kathy L., and Terrell, Stephen J. *Nurturing Resilience: Helping Clients Move Forward from Developmental Trauma—An Integrative Somatic Approach*. North Atlantic Books, 2018.

5   I heard the phrase "dose the field" from somatic attachment therapist, Diane Poole Heller. The way I use the phrase, the "field" is the ritual space that encompasses the physical, emotional, psychological, and energetic dimensions. Whenever we sense a contraction in the body, we slow down to dose the field with more safeness before proceeding. We might put on a sweater, take a sip of water, lock the door, allow ourselves to rock from side to side for a while, call in a different protective ally from the spirit realm, visualize a pink bubble of protection around us, or simply pause for a while to settle the breath and come back to noticing the most relaxed part of the body.

6   Rubinstein, D., and Lahad, M. "Fantastic Reality: The Role of Imagination, Playfulness, and Creativity in Healing Trauma." *Traumatology* 29, no. 2 (2023): 102–11. https://doi.org/10.1037/trm0000376.

Hill-Jarrett, T. G. "The Black Radical Imagination: A Space of Hope and Possible Futures." *Frontiers in Neurology* 14 (September 22, 2023): 1241922. DOI: 10.3389/fneur.2023.1241922.

Kapitan, Lynn, PhD, ATR-BC. "The Empathic Imagination of Art Therapy: Good for the Brain?" *Art Therapy* 27, no. 4 (2010): 158–59. DOI: 10.1080/07421656.2010.10129384.

Brugnoli, Maria Paola. "Spiritual Healing in Palliative Care with Clinical Hypnosis: Neuroscience and Therapy." *American Journal of Clinical Hypnosis* (2023). DOI: 10.1080/00029157.2023.2281466.

7   This is a sneaky way that appropriation can creep into your spiritual practice. Remember: It's spiritual/cultural appreciation if you have a connection to a wisdom holder who has freely given you information with intent to support your practice, and you use your practice to empower and uplift marginalized communities. It's appropriation if you don't acknowledge that the practice originates in a marginalized community, or if your use of the knowledge commodifies that culture for your own benefit or perpetuates stereotypes about the community. Hint: If you don't know the origin of the practice, you are in commodification territory. Which elements are important in your heritage? This is a great research and ancestral healing opportunity!

8   I apologize in advance to all the editors, copyeditors, and grammar lovers that I'm going to drive nuts with my "inconsistent" capitalization in this book. Here is my suggestion for an animist style guide: When referring to the oversoul of a conventionally improper noun, it may be capitalized to elevate status and meaning from general to specific honorific. Oversoul here means the highest collective spiritual essence of the group to which this noun is a member. In a very small way, we're rewilding the style guide. In a paragraph that mentions plastics a dozen times, there may be a single instance where I refer to capital "P" Plastic. At that moment in the material, I'm asking the reader to cast awareness a little wider and orient to the highest spiritual essence of the subject matter; I'm asking you to consider the oversoul of Plastic.

In other words, sometimes I'll capitalize nouns to indicate an animist relationship that includes the soul and spirit of this being, its folklore and mythology, and a lived experience in relationship with them. Using proper noun status extends my meaning beyond their fixed location on the material plane. It implies the oversoul and multidimensionality of that plant, animal, or elemental group. It's like the difference between saying "my spiritual community" versus "Quakers." The latter paints a much richer picture with specific details. It is also a sign of respect.

If it's not capitalized, I'm referring more generally to something, however, I always try to remember, "Nature is not universal or common, but unique to a specific worldview that came about at a particular time for specific reasons." For more, see Liboiron, Max. *Pollution Is Colonialism*. Duke University Press, 2021.

Sometimes I will choose not to capitalize only because it can overwhelm on the page, particularly when I'm writing a long list. Know that this is meant as a neurologic rest, not to indicate a lesser degree of honor or respect.

9   Butler, Octavia E. *Parable of the Sower*. Grand Central Publishing, 2023.

10 The book you hold has very much been shaped by Butler, Octavia E. *Parable of the Sower*. Grand Central Publishing, 2023. Some may find it too grim. Most find it chillingly accurate. I find it comforting.

11 Said every human in every era.

12 The Statue of Unity is the world's largest bronze statue. It is located in Gujurat, India.

13 Liboiron, Max. *Pollution Is Colonialism*. Duke University Press, 2021.

14 John Mellencamp.

15 "World egg." Wikipedia, The Free Encyclopedia. Wikimedia Foundation, Inc. Accessed February 25, 2024. https://en.wikipedia.org/wiki/World_egg.

    Wikipedia contributors. "Musica Universalis." Wikipedia, The Free Encyclopedia. Accessed January 11, 2024. https://en.wikipedia.org/wiki/Musica_universalis.

16 It wasn't a cliché until a New Age Movement's worth of white people yoga dharma talks, logo coffee mugs, and slogan T-shirts picked up the phrase and ran with it after Carl Sagan, in his famous television series *Cosmos: A Personal Voyage*, popularized this idea with his statement: "The nitrogen in our DNA, the calcium in our teeth, the iron in our blood, the carbon in our apple pies were made in the interiors of collapsing stars. We are made of starstuff."

17 I first heard a discussion of "satisfiability" in a workshop led by Staci Haines, generative somatics instructor and author of *The Politics of Trauma*. I became fascinated by the concept, immediately sensing it was a core skill for collapse resilience. I began to include it in my teaching and public speaking, including my Collapse 101 course. Some

years after the publication of adrienne maree brown's book, *Pleasure Activism,* I discovered in its pages that they, too, discuss it at length in their work. I highly recommend their books for deeper exploration.

Haines, Staci. *The Politics of Trauma: Somatics, Healing, and Social Justice.* North Atlantic Books, 2019.

brown, adrienne maree. *Pleasure Activism: The Politics of Feeling Good.* AK Press, 2019.

18   Essential reading to illuminate the ways in which therapy is—and has always been—political: see Mullan, Jennifer. *Decolonizing Therapy: Oppression, Historical Trauma, and Politicizing Your Practice.* W. W. Norton, 2023.

For an introduction to polyvagal theory: Dana, Deborah. *Anchored: How to Befriend Your Nervous System Using Polyvagal Theory.* Sounds True, 2021.

For beginner's attachment theory: Poole Heller, Diane. *The Power of Attachment: How to Create Deep and Lasting Intimate Relationships.* Sounds True, 2019.

For the basics of ritual in ecofeminist witchcraft: Starhawk and Valentine, Hillary. *The Twelve Wild Swans.* HarperCollins, 2000.

For a deeper dive into personal mythwork: Estés, Clarissa Pinkola. *Women Who Run with the Wolves.* Random House Publishing Group, 1995.

For deeper exploration of ritual and seasonality: Spagnola, Carmen. *The Spirited Kitchen: Recipes and Rituals for the Wheel of the Year.* Countryman Press, 2022.

To understand the interlocking systems of oppression that form the basis of the modern witch archetype, this is essential reading: Federici, Silvia. *Caliban and the Witch: Women, the Body, and Primitive Accumulation.* Autonomedia, 2004.

19   "Power Threat Meaning Framework (PTMF)." The British Psychological Society, accessed October 22, 2023. https://www.bps.org.uk/member-networks/division-clinical-psychology/power-threat-meaning-framework.

20   For more on matching rituals to seasons: Foster, Steven, and Little, Meredith. *The Four Shields: The Initiatory Seasons of Human Nature.* Lost Borders Press, 1999.

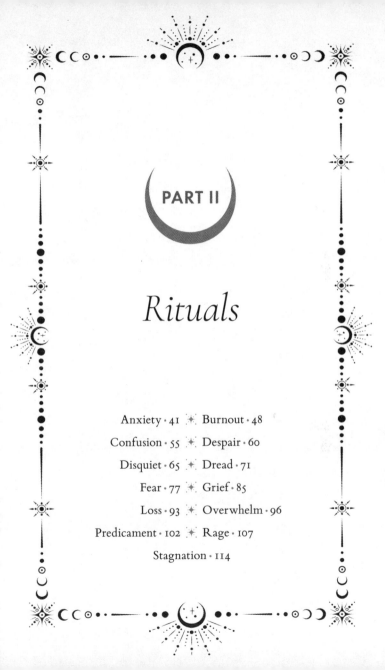

PART II

Rituals

Anxiety · 41 ✦ Burnout · 48

Confusion · 55 ✦ Despair · 60

Disquiet · 65 ✦ Dread · 71

Fear · 77 ✦ Grief · 85

Loss · 93 ✦ Overwhelm · 96

Predicament · 102 ✦ Rage · 107

Stagnation · 114

Anxiety

Sacred Writing

Let's dive right in, shall we? How's your Anxiety level living in late-stage racialized capitalism, after years of global pandemic and escalating climate chaos, with social tension like a tightly coiled spring wound to its maximum limit ready to release its pent-up energy in an unpredictable and tumultuous burst? Hmm?

Okay, but seriously, Anxiety is a major problem so it deserves a robust Ritual. Very few of the Rituals in this book are as involved as this one, but since Anxiety can be so powerful and intense, it gets a more fulsome ritual container.

Research has shown that a form of expressive writing can help with symptoms of anxiety, depression, and PTSD.[1] In this Ritual, we combine therapeutic journaling with another technique from expressive arts therapy that is designed to externalize our Anxiety.

Anxiety is not who we are. It's not a fixed identity. Anxiety is a problem, and while our lives and our comportment may be dominated and highly shaped by this problem, it is not our Self. Anxiety is a shitty little tyrant that mercilessly tortures us. It acts like it's protecting us, but its heavy-handedness and overbearing nature is suffocating. We are not the problem, Anxiety is. We are a perfectly lovely human. We are just a little mammal making our way in a scary world. It's reasonable to worry sometimes. It is unreasonable to have our mind and body constantly under the command of a tyrant who never listens to us.

SPIRITUAL POWER TOOLS

Talisman: An object you create to represent and harness specific energies. Wands, poppets, corn dollies, certain forms of regalia, and spiritual jewelry are all examples.

Amulet: A found object with its own special quality and inherent significance, such as a lucky penny, a rock in the shape of a heart, or an eagle feather.

Fetish: A single-use object that you could burn, bury, throw, flush, or otherwise dispose.

In this ritual, you'll use a talisman to house your Anxiety. When Anxiety is properly placed outside of ourselves, we gain perspective and a bit of breathing room (sometimes literally!). Take a deep breath now at the thought of Anxiety removed from you and located outside of yourself. *Ahhhhhhh* . . . shoulders dropping, eyebrows relaxing, jaw unclenching, belly releasing now. . . . If you want, you can jettison your talisman when you're done.

You should know in advance that this ritual may make you feel a bit worse before you feel better. Honestly, it's just not that fun to hang out with Anxiety for an extended period of time. This Ritual is spread out over four days, but the active time for each writing session should be just 10 to 20 minutes each day. Watch for holding your breath, contracted posture, headache, or other signs that the tension is too much. If you experience any of these symptoms, or any other physical manifestations of acute discomfort or distress, don't try to "push through." Just end the ritual.

Keep this one short and sweet, but perhaps don't avoid it altogether. If your everyday reality is essentially governed by a shitty little tyrant, then maybe it's time to just have it out with them.

TIMING

You can do this ritual anytime, but not on a day when you have an important obligation directly afterward. Make sure you schedule time for aftercare immediately after your journaling session. It will be helpful to move your arms and legs, so plan to spend as much time afterward either walking or doing a relaxing task as you did for your journal writing.

SUPPLIES

- A doll, either folksy and homemade from scraps of fabric or a thrift shop find
- Paper and pen
- An uplifting essential oil

1. Make a doll or pick one up at the thrift shop to represent your Anxiety. Give it a name like Shitty Little Tyrant, Mean Bossman, Gloomy Roomie, Tammy, Dave, or just Anxiety. Place it on your writing desk with you.

2. Sit with your Anxiety doll, writing implements, and essential oil in front of you. Ideally, you'll use a pen and paper to get the full benefit of handwriting, which promotes sensory engagement and calms the brain, versus a keyboard, which can be associated with work stress. Imagine you can see currents of anxious energy in the air, like an electric storm. Open the bottle of essential oil and take a whiff. As you breathe in the soothing aroma, visualize the anxious energy becoming smoother, like gentle waves or a calming breeze. Reseal the lid if you prefer.

3. Set a timer for 10 to 20 minutes. Write to Anxiety and share your thoughts and feelings with them. Try not to lose yourself in your feelings and relive them. Simply be frank and honest with Anxiety about how they

make you feel. Tell them what they rob you of and how they affect your self-image. You may feel anger, bitterness, or resentment. You also might feel some gratitude for ways in which Anxiety keeps you safe. There's no right or wrong way to feel about them. Simply list how you've been impacted by Anxiety and what it's been like for you. How have they influenced your relationships, career, health, and self-image?[2]

When the timer goes off, put your pen down. Stretch, shake off any heaviness, get up and move around a bit.[3]

Put your Anxiety doll away somewhere out of sight until tomorrow.

4. Set another timer for 15 minutes. Dedicate this time to your aftercare. Perhaps make yourself a hot cup of tea with honey.

5. The next day, repeat steps 2 and 3, but this time tell Anxiety about a specific time they fucked you over. Write for 10 to 20 minutes, then spend 15 minutes in aftercare.

6. The following day, repeat the process again. This time, imagine who you would be without Anxiety dominating so much of your time and energy. Write for 10 to 20 minutes, then spend 15 minutes in aftercare.

7. On the last day, write about how you would like to proceed in a relationship with Anxiety. Dream about the possibilities of a new dynamic, even if it's only slightly different. Write for 10 to 20 minutes, then spend 15 minutes in aftercare.

At the end of the final sacred writing session, decide what to do with your Anxiety doll. Do you want to release them? Honor them? Give them a glow up? Should you cleanse them with disinfectant and positive vibes, and donate them back to the thrift shop? You get to decide how you'll move forward, with or without your old friend, Anxiety.[4]

PROTECT YOUR HEART

Expressive writing can trigger a sense of shame and embarrassment. The fear of someone reading your private thoughts can create internal resistance to writing things down. You may want to burn your writing directly afterward.

Author's Notes

1   Expressive writing was developed by James Pennebaker and John Evans. It is sometimes called therapeutic journaling. A 2012 meta-analysis investigating the efficacy of expressive writing for treatment of acute stress disorder, PTSD, and depression, resulted in significant and substantial short-term reductions in symptoms. The researchers concluded that expressive writing could provide a useful tool to promote mental health with only minimal contact with a therapist. Pennebaker, J. W., and Chung, C. K. "Expressive Writing: Connections to Physical and Mental Health." In *Oxford Handbook of Health Psychology*, edited by H. S. Friedman. Oxford University Press, 2011.

2   Once you begin writing, write continuously without stopping. Don't worry about spelling or grammar. If you run out of things to say, simply repeat what you have already written. Keep writing about the topic until the time is up.

3   Writing exercises aren't for everyone. If this Ritual evokes strong feelings that you cannot cope with, stop immediately and do something soothing for yourself. Experiencing symptoms of hypervigilance or acute distress are signals to discontinue this practice. Take care of yourself by doing something like diaphragmatic breathing, or simply stand up and walk forward while you look forward. This signals to your body and mind that you are not prey, and recruits your legs, arms, and eyes into the task of scanning for safeness and resources in the environment.

4   If you're one of the people intrepidly reading the book front to back, how about taking a break right now? Stand up, stretch, poke your head out the window for some fresh air. I'm serious, you should not consume therapeutic material like it's sweet and salty caramel popcorn. Tear yourself away, please, even if it's just to look up from the page and focus on the middle distance for a few moments.

Burnout

Floating in the Vastness

If we weren't already hanging on by a thread, operating well beyond our capacity to cope with life in late-stage racialized capitalism amid escalating climate emergencies, then certainly the global pandemic pushed most of us over the threshold. Burnout has become a bit of a buzzword, but it's more than just chronic weariness and fatigue. Burnout is characterized by chronic stress that is not alleviated with a good night's sleep or by taking it easy over the weekend.

The root causes of Burnout include unfair treatment, unmanageable workload, and unreasonable time pressure. In the workplace, lack of support and poor communication skills by supervisors are main contributors. Autistic burnout is caused by the stress of masking to survive in an unaccommodating neurotypical world and involves exhaustion, withdrawal, reduced cognitive function, increased struggles with the daily tasks of living, and exacerbation of autistic traits.[1] Black women, who not-so-coincidentally also experience higher rates of heart disease and greater intensity of hot flashes during the menopausal transition, are literally 7.5 years biologically "older" than white women due to social, economic, and environmental factors that lead to burnout.[2, 3]

What I've noticed with Burnout is that the emotional exhaustion is so pervasive that any little random thing can cause utter breakdown. Dysregulation is constant, resilience is totally depleted, coping skills are nonexistent. Tears arise over seemingly small disappointments. There can be a numbness and fogginess that persists for months. In my experience with clients, when people get to the depersonalization and derealization stage (the persistent feeling that you're outside your body or like the world isn't quite real and time isn't functioning normally), we're looking at a multiyear recovery process that's sometimes hindered by stress-related onset of autoimmune disease.[4]

Probably the hardest part of this ritual is making time to actually do it. There are reasons you're burnt out. Time pressure is real! I totally understand. I can't tell you how to prioritize yourself. I just know that if you're burnt out, you're running out of options. If you don't make time for your care, well . . . statistically, certain outcomes are more likely for you than others. Please make time for this.

It's worth repeating here that magic on its own is not going to fix the oppressive conditions that cause Burnout.

However, summoning support from the Greater Than Human can be helpful toward this goal. It's going to take a big dose of magic to create the world we want to live in. So first things first: let's be real and acknowledge just how bad it really is. Once you see the situation accurately, you might notice feelings of grief, fear, or despair come up. Let's focus the magic there and create a supportive container to dream something new into being.

Though your Burnout may not cause the sensation of heat in your body, Burnout is associated with systemic inflammation, so we'll want as much water as possible for this ritual, enough to completely immerse yourself.[5] If you're lucky enough to be able to treat yourself to a session in one of those private float pods and you're not claustrophobic, yay for you! If you live near the Ocean and it's warm enough, you could do a float ritual there. You could do this one at your local swimming pool if there are quiet hours and it feels safe to be in public. Or you could do it in your bathtub at home. If you're uncomfortable immersed in water, how about just your feet? The temperature of the water is purely your preference, though I'd suggest that cooler is better from the perspective of sympathetic magic: We want to quell the fiery energies that are consuming your Spirit.

TIMING
You can do this ritual anytime and as often as you need.

SUPPLIES
- Enough water to immerse yourself in

1. Take yourself to the water and sit for a moment, just observing it. Remember how humans evolved from ancient aquatic ancestors, all the way back to the single cell ones. From this basic life-form flowed everything else you can remember and everything around you now. Sit with the Vastness of Potential for a moment. If it feels overwhelming, imagine a protective and nurturing guide sitting beside you.

2. Invoke the Vastness. Pray to it for an increase in support, intercession, energy, capacity, resilience, power, whatever you need. It might sound like, "Great Vastness, I beseech you. You who are all things, please send me _____."

3. Make a simple offering to the Vastness. Make it small and personal. An eyelash, a single strand of hair, blow a kiss. Your DNA identifies you. Because it's tiny, it sends the message: *I'm so small and you're so immense. I know my place in the cosmic order. I also know my problem is so much bigger than myself. Only something even greater and more powerful will help.*

4. In one word, name a root cause of your Burnout. For example, "work" or "manager." Use your fin-

ger to write that word on the palm of your hand, as though you were writing with invisible ink. Keep listing causes and writing them down in the palm of your hand.

5. Enter the water and turn onto your back. Open your palms to the sky. Release these root causes to the Vastness. Imagine them dissolving into the Vastness. Feel the water washing them away. Verbally affirm this release. *Take them from me. I let them go. I banish them. I release them. I release them. I release them.*

6. Float for a while, allowing yourself to be held and the Burnout to be tempered by the Vastness. Ask the Vastness to show you other ways of being, new modes of functioning, alternate worlds of care and dignity where Burnout doesn't exist for you anymore. . . . Let yourself float and be dreamy for a while. Affirm your visions of potential and possibility by repeating to yourself, "Yes, yes, yes, please and thank you."

7. As you emerge from the water, remember to offer gratitude to the Vastness.

8. After you've dried yourself off but before you move on to the next part of your day, remember some of the visions of alternate possibilities you had while you

were floating. Name them and write them down in the palm of your hand. Squeeze them into your palm, and cup your other hand around it. Hold on to them for a moment. Now press your palm to your heart and press the possibilities deeper into you whenever you need to connect with them. You carry these possibilities with you now, into the rest of your day, and whenever you need a reminder you can simply place your hand on your heart and feel the Vastness of Potential within you.

Author's Notes

....

1   Higgins, J. M., Arnold, S. R., Weise, J., Pellicano, E., and Trollor, J. N. "Defining Autistic Burnout Through Experts by Lived Experience: Grounded Delphi Method Investigating #AutisticBurnout." *Autism* 25, no. 8 (2021): 2356–69. DOI: 10.1177/13623613211019858.

2   A 2022 study by Aflac Insurance found that 71 percent of Gen Z, 69 percent of Hispanic people, 65 percent of millennials, 57 percent of Gen X, 62 percent of women, and 57 percent of men reported currently experiencing at least moderate levels of burnout. Alarmingly, since 2020 the rates of burnout have gotten worse, not better. Aflac. "Employee Well-Being and Mental Health." *Aflac WorkForces Report.* 2022–2023. Accessed February 7, 2024. https://www.aflac .com/docs/awr/pdf/2022-trends-and-topics/2022-aflac-awr-employee -well-being-and-mental-health.pdf.

3   Geronimus, Arline T., Hicken, Margaret T., Pearson, Jay A., Seashols, Sarah J., Brown, Kelly L., and Cruz, Tracey D. "Do US Black Women Experience Stress-Related Accelerated Biological Aging?:

A Novel Theory and First Population-Based Test of Black-White Differences in Telomere Length." *Human Nature* 21, no. 1 (2010): 19–38. DOI: 10.1007/s12110-010-9078-0.

Felix, A. S., Lehman, A., Nolan, T. S., Sealy-Jefferson, S., Breathett, K., Hood, D. B., Addison, D., Anderson, C. M., Cené, C. W., Warren, B. J., Jackson, R. D., and Williams, K. P. "Stress, Resilience, and Cardiovascular Disease Risk Among Black Women." *Circulation: Cardiovascular Quality and Outcomes*, 12, no. 4 (2019): e005284. https://doi.org/10.1161/CIRCOUTCOMES.118.005284.

4   Song, H., Fang, F., Tomasson, G., et al. "Association of Stress-Related Disorders with Subsequent Autoimmune Disease." *JAMA* 319, no. 23 (2018): 2388–2400. DOI: 10.1001/jama.2018.7028.

5   Adebayo, Oladimeji, Nkhata, Misheck J, Kanmodi, Kehinde K., Alatishe, Taiwo, Egbedina, Eyinade, Ojo, Temitope, Ojedokun, Samson, Oladapo, John, Moshood Adeoye, Abiodun, and Nnyanzi, Lawrence A. "Relationship between Burnout, Cardiovascular Risk Factors, and Inflammatory Markers: A Protocol for Scoping Review" *Journal of Molecular Pathology* 4, no. 3 (2023): 189–95. DOI: 10.3390/jmp4030017.

Confusion

Truth Wheel

Confusion, and its meeker cousin ambivalence, often lead to stuckness, stagnation, and low-key freeze response. It takes some courage to address Confusion. It's a blurry state that often serves as cover for other more intense and even less desirable states. Underneath confusion often lies fear, anger, and grief.

I don't want to imply that confusion is always unwarranted. Not at all. I mean, living in these times? Confusion is most definitely warranted. It's hard to know what to prioritize, who to believe, how to stay balanced. Confusion is the natural response to unsolvable problems and, frankly, a lot of our problems are unsolvable. How are we supposed to heal ecosystems and social disparities inside a capitalist system? That's a real head scratcher![1]

I think we should respect Confusion as a warning sign. It signals a need to slow down, cast our awareness a little wider, and be brave enough to acknowledge what else is also present when Confusion enters the room. Confusion asks us to dig deeper until we reach some fundamental truths. This Truth Wheel ritual provides a process for nuanced inquiry.[2]

TIMING

Anytime, but especially during the Dark Moon phase (the three days leading up to a New Moon). Things are often unclear during this phase, so it's not a great time for magic or divination, but it can be the perfect time to explore the unconscious. Think of this period as a fertile void where unnamed and excluded parts of our problem wait to be discovered.

SUPPLIES

- A timer
- Whatever you need to make a large circle on the ground with a smaller circle in the center,[3] divided into quadrants, like this Truth Wheel image:

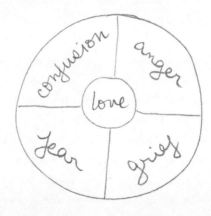

- Objects to represent Anger, Fear, Grief, Confusion, and Love.[4] Some people like to use Hope in the center of the circle instead of Love. Use whichever concept most closely approximates for you an ideal state of well-being, acceptance, nurturance, belonging, and support.

1. Delineate your Truth Wheel on the ground or floor.

2. Place Love at the center. Add your objects for Confusion, Anger, Grief, and Fear, each in their own section of the big wheel, intuitively selecting which one goes where.

3. Set a timer for 10 to 20 minutes. It should be a length of time that feels slightly longer than you would prefer. If your instinct is 15 minutes, try 17. Don't punish yourself, but a little challenge is probably good if you tend to avoid these emotions.[5]

4. Take a few breaths to ground yourself. Notice the air in your lungs, the rise and fall of your chest. Feel yourself on solid ground. Focus for a moment on the supportive energies surrounding you. What's good? Once you feel resourced enough, turn on the timer and place yourself in the quadrant of Confusion. Just be there with Confusion for this period of time, sitting or standing, moving or still. What sensations and

emotions arise? Is there a movement or sound that expresses how you feel?

5. When the timer goes off, do some arm sweeps to brush off Confusion, running your palm down your arm from shoulder to fingertips. Shake your body like a dog coming out of the water. Step out of Confusion and into the next quadrant that calls you. (If you need a break first, please do that.)

   For each quadrant you'll follow the same process: What sensations and emotions arise? Do these sensations or emotions make you want to express somehow with movement or sound? What's it like to fully step into this experience? Do any insights come?

6. The last section you'll enter is the innermost circle of the wheel, Love. Feel free to rest here for as long as you like, absorbing the varied energies of Love, both cosmic and personal.

7. When the last timer sounds, offer thanks to all the helpers in the unseen realms who supported you during this ritual. Step out of your Truth Wheel with more clarity around how you think and feel.

Author's Notes

1   We can't.

2   Thanks to Sparrow Hart for introducing me to this ritual.

3   I've only ever done this ritual outdoors where I can mark a big circle in the dirt. However, it could easily be done indoors so long as you have some way of marking the floor. Your wheel could be made of mundane items such as masking tape, string, or dominoes, or as clever and beautiful as a mandala of found objects.

4   If that feels too hard, write those words down on scraps of paper. If you're out in nature, you could use a prickly vine or a sharp stick to represent Anger. Perhaps a very heavy black rock could be Grief. Maybe a chaotic-looking branch could stand in for Confusion. A heart-shaped leaf for Love.

5   If you're the type who's more likely to linger and lose yourself in the vortex of these emotions, then knock a couple minutes off. For you, less is more with this one. Your timer is going to help reinforce the sacred container of this ritual. Please don't do this freestyle—be disciplined about time. You're going to repeat this amount of time four times, once for each outer section of the wheel.

Despair

The Goddess in the Hole

Despair feels so heavy and pervasive that it's hard to imagine any ritual offering relief. Despair is an appropriate response to our times. To relieve Despair altogether is not only impossible but, I believe, ill-advised; to live with Despair is a signal that our humanity, however disillusioned, still rests on the belief that the world can and should be better.

To be clear: There's no shame in not feeling able to live with Despair. I do wish, though, that each of us were witnessed in our Despair. I wish us all to have companionship in our Despair, and dignity, and the solace of someone to listen to our heartache.

I once attended a fascinating lecture on the Bronze Age worship of a Sun-and-Earth goddess in Anatolia, a possible ancestor to the Greek goddess, Hekate.[1] The ancient Hittites used to dig holes on the sides of riverbanks to represent a gateway to the Underworld. There they would leave offerings to the goddess. They placed dollhouse-size beds and ladders for her, and keys to represent her role as gatekeeper to the realm of the ancestors and primordial powers. They made ears out of pottery and placed them in the hole believing she could hear their prayers.

When I think of ancient humans surviving ice ages, catastrophic earthquakes and tsunamis, brutal wars with rudimentary medicine and surgery, malnutrition, famine and devastating plagues, the collapse of empires and complex societies, I feel more than just Despair. I feel wonder and awe and disbelief. I can't imagine how they did it. Yet, humans are still here. Against all odds, beyond all understanding, we've somehow survived a never-ending onslaught of peril.

I imagine ancient people performing rituals like this, leaving offerings to The Goddess in the Hole, because with no escape from their circumstances they were desperate for divine intercession. It seems like this is the type of thing humans do in our collective foxhole moments—we plead with the gods of mercy to help us out. There is some comfort in the idea that there are Others in the Unseen Realms who listen and absorb our Despair, hold it with us, without judgement or diminishment, steadfast guardians of our innermost truth.

TIMING

This ritual is a good candidate for a regular Waning or Balsamic Crescent Moon practice, the time of dissolving into darkness, the crucible of rest and recuperation.

Those of us born during a Waning Crescent Moon tend to be somewhat oriented to collapse and endings, and are often pretty good at allowing change to arrive. Others might consider us a bit of a gloomy bunch, but we're not. We just relish in poignance.

If you don't have a natural affinity for endings, release, and lingering with Despair, the Waning Crescent Moon phase can support you and help hold this ritual for you.

SUPPLIES

- Something to dig with and a private place to do it
- Offerings to the Gatekeeper of the Underworld such as dollhouse furniture, an earring, a key, food or drink
- An uncooked egg

1. Dig a hole and place inside your offerings to The Goddess in the Hole, Gatekeeper to the Underworld.

2. Sitting or lying beside the hole, turn your face toward it and speak your Despair into the earth. Let your words and tears flow freely; they are both petition and offering.

3. When your speaking feels complete, place the egg in the hole. This represents the Cosmic Egg, an ancient mythological symbol for a new world that emerges out of darkness and chaos.

4. Decide whether you want to bury your offerings to the Gatekeeper or remove them to reuse in the future. Fill in the hole, covering the egg as you would a seed.

AFTERCARE: Soon after working with Despair, I'd advise you to work with two remedies that don't have their own chapters in this book but deserve some attention here: Agency and World-Building. This can be as simple as watching a movie or reading a book where the characters take back their power and their future. Sci-fi and fantasy are great for this. Let yourself be inspired by depictions of the irrepressible human spirit.[2]

If you like to write or draw, create the future you wish for in great detail. Daydream about it. Immerse yourself in a scenario where you are the protagonist with a first-person point of view. You have control over actions and consequences. As Joan Baez said, "Action is the antidote to despair."

Author's Notes

1   University of Victoria. "Cavi Lecture: Professor Mary Bach-varova." Last modified October 16, 2023. Accessed February 7, 2024. https://www.uvic.ca/humanities/greekroman/home/news/archive/cavi_lecture_professor_mary_bachvarova,_thursday,_18_oct._730_pm,_cle_a212.php.

2   Studies by the UC Berkeley's Greater Good Science Center found that a daily dose of inspiration correlates to increased capacity for positive emotion, buffers against feelings of social disconnectedness, and helps with motivation. These small inputs of focused attention on Agency and World-Building can lead to a revolution from within that ripples out into your everyday life. Pinterest. "Pinterest releases new research with UC Berkeley's Greater Good Science Center." Accessed February 7, 2024. https://business.pinterest.com/en-ca/blog/positivity-research-pinterest-berkeley/.

Disquiet

Altar to Cassandra

In Greek mythology, the god Apollo gives a mortal, Cassandra, the gift of prophecy. When she later refuses his sexual advances, he becomes angry and sabotages her with the curse of never being believed. She tries to warn people that the Trojan horse is a trick, that Troy will fall, Odysseus will wander for more than a decade, and alerts many others to their impending doom. While each of her predictions come true, she is ignored and unfairly cast as a madwoman, causing her endless pain and frustration.

I know the feeling.

As someone who's been tracking the converging emergencies of large scale environmental and social collapse for a long time, I'll raise my hand and say, *I am Cassandra.* Climate scientists alerting us to catastrophic climate change for multiple decades are Cassandra. Folks with invisible illness or disability: Cassandra. Any victim of sexual assault who's heard the reply, *He's always been nice to me . . .* Cassandra. People with mental illness who speak out against carceral medical care . . . trans people who warn us about escalating judicial attacks on bodily autonomy . . . historians who decry the modern resurrection of fascism . . . whistleblowers in the government, the military, corporations, and the medical industry . . . all are afflicted with the Cassandra Complex.

In 1988, psychoanalyst Laurie Layton Schapira wrote that the Cassandra Complex involves three main features: encounters with patriarchy, women's emotional or physical suffering, and disbelief when sufferers attempt to relay their experiences to institutions.[1]

No one wants to listen to Cassandra because to do so requires us to go against the social tide. Few people willingly trade in the comfort and safety of belonging for outsider status. Denial protects us from anxiety, guilt, and the personal risks of moral action.

But to deny our Disquiet and ignore our instincts brings ruin all the same. We either speak our truth and are branded hysterical and sidelined or we eat our words and hope they don't rot our insides. The curse of not being believed is almost as bad as the pain of not speaking up. Cassandra has been described as one of those "who often combine deep, true insight with utter helplessness, and who retreat into madness."

But who is really cursed here, Cassandra or the people who don't listen to her when her predictions invariably come true? Personally, I'm Team Cassandra all the way.[2]

To create your altar to Cassandra, you'll need to assemble a few items to represent her. Her stories are rich with symbols and associations from which to draw inspiration. She was protected by Athena, the goddess of wisdom, often represented by an owl. As children, she and her brother were left in the temple where they were enveloped by snakes who whispered in their ears, enabling the young ones to hear the future. When Cassandra tried to warn her countrymen that the Greeks were hiding in ambush inside the Trojan horse, they laughed at her. She took up an axe and a burning torch and ran at the horse, intent on revealing the truth. She was subdued by soldiers, but meanwhile, inside the Trojan horse, the Greeks trembled at their near exposure. Because so many of her predictions involve the death of her suitors and family members, skulls would be appropriate.[3]

You can also include any individual who in your view embodies the Cassandra Complex. Write their name on a slip of paper or print off a picture of them. People who come to mind for me include prescient authors, Octavia Butler and Ursula Le Guin, trailblazing crip and disability rights advocates, Alice Wong, Mia Mingus, and Judy Heumann, and iconic truth tellers, Anita Hill and Christine Blasey Ford.

Also choose an item to represent the Current Troubling Situation about which you feel Disquiet, foreboding, or an inner knowing that disturbs you. For instance, if a headline from the news has triggered this feeling, print off a screenshot. If you're worried about a climate disaster like wildfire, use a piece of charred wood. If no object feels appropriate, you can simply write a few descriptive words on a piece of paper—the who, what, when, where, and why.

TIMING
The time for this ritual is sooner than later. Possibly always. It's never a bad time to acknowledge Disquiet.

SUPPLIES
- An item (or several) to represent Cassandra, such as an owl, snake, horse, axe, torch, or skull
- An item to represent your Current Troubling Situation
- A candle
- An offering to Cassandra, for instance a morsel of food, a drink, pinch of incense, or a song

1. Delineate a sacred space for your altar to Cassandra. This could be the top of a dresser, a bookshelf, a fancy tray, or a box covered with a pretty piece of fabric. Create your altar with a symbol of Cassandra occupying prime real estate. Place your symbol of the Current Troubling Situation in front of her.

2. Light a candle and welcome Cassandra to this ritual in her honor.

3. Make an offering to her of food, drink, incense, or song, whatever you feel moved to give.

4. For a few moments, simply acknowledge her suffering. Empathize with her madness and frustration. Make space inside yourself for her. Thank her for speaking her truth. Let her know, *I hear you. I believe you. I witness your courage. You are not alone.*

5. Imagine Cassandra speaks to you. What would she say to you about your Disquiet? Feel the energy of her message to you: *I hear you. I believe you. I witness your courage. You are not alone.*

6. Ask Cassandra for what you need, be it strength, stamina, decisiveness, calm, confidence, or a clear sign to help you know what to do with your Disquiet. Use your inhale to receive her support deep into your body. Thank her before you blow out the candle to signal the close of the Ritual.

Author's Notes

1   Schapira, Laurie Layton. *The Cassandra Complex: Living with Disbelief: a Modern Perspective on Hysteria.* Inner City Books, 1988.

2   Join Team Cassandra—we're more fun than we seem! We can get T-shirts! Learn more about the Cassandra Complex: "Cassandra (metaphor)." Wikipedia. Last modified July 17, 2023. Accessed October 17, 2023. https://en.wikipedia.org/wiki/Cassandra_(metaphor).

    Eichenlaub, Constance. "In the Shadow of Power and Eros: The Cassandra Complex and Psychic Numbing." In *Unity and Diversity in Religion and Culture: Exploring the Psychological and Philosophical Issues Underlying Global Conflict,* edited by International Readings on Theory, History and Philosophy of Culture, XXII, 125–29. Eidos, 2006. Accessed November 7, 2023. http://www.spbric.org/PDF/pub_edin.pdf. Eighth International Conference on Philosophy and Culture, *Unity and Diversity in Religion* (2005).

    Ratcliffe, Krista. "Listening to Cassandra: A Materialist-Feminist Exposé of the Necessary Relations Between Rhetoric and Hermaneutics." *Marquette University e-Publications@Marquette, English Faculty Research and Publications* (1995). Accessed January 8, 2024.

3   For a jaw-dropping example of art-as-altar, check out Judy Chicago's feminist masterpiece, *The Dinner Party* at the Brooklyn Museum. Cassandra is grouped under Sophia on one of the nameplates on the Heritage Floor, along with other negated women dismissed throughout history.

    Brooklyn Museum. "Sophia: The Dinner Party." Accessed *January* 10, 2024. https://www.brooklynmuseum.org/eascfa/dinner_party/place_settings/sophia.

Dread

Date with Cold Reality

Dread is a visceral experience. Its nauseating presence forms a grim backdrop to life that makes it difficult to focus or function. Of all the freeze-inducing emotions, Dread—a sickening combination of fear, anxiety, anticipation, and expectation—is perhaps the most torturous.

Science has long known that the anticipation of pain can be as painful as pain itself, firing some of the same regions in the brain.[1] Time and Dread are dysfunctional together. We aren't going to notice if we bang our elbow running out of a burning building, just as I'm not worried enough about developing dementia in the future to stop myself from eating a pound of sugary gummy candies to distract myself from uncomfortable feelings in the present.[2] However, as a dreaded event approaches, the angst intensifies. Yet, if we put off the event, we have more time to feel uncertain and wobbly about whether we can tolerate the outcome, which only compounds the Dread.[3]

A constant low-grade state of Dread is practically an archetypal experience of apocalypse. For years, I've dreaded climate change feedback loops and tipping points, and now I dread wildly fluctuating climate chaos. I used to dread aging and death. Now I dread that many of us will not die of natural causes in old age, but rather of (once-preventable) disasters of human-caused climate chaos, novel disease, and crumbling healthcare systems. Moreover, the "us" who'll suffer this tragic injustice will disproportionately be People of the Global Majority (Black, Indigenous, and People of Color) living close to the equator. Dread is an acute sense of our lack of control, of catastrophic potential, fatal consequences, and inequitable distribution of risk.

I think now is a good time to pause and take a breath. I'm crying, you're shocked how quickly this went dark, and we're both feeling tense. Let's put this book down for a moment and have a little release. Slow your breathing and focus on the exhale.

Whew. Okay. We can handle this. Here's what we're gonna do:

TIMING

There's a preparation phase to this ritual, and it will take as long as it takes for your body to acclimate. It's an import-

Do not do this ritual, or any kind of cold-water immersion, if you are pregnant or if you have a heart-related condition such as:

- High blood pressure
- Diabetes
- Heart disease
- Peripheral neuropathy
- Poor blood circulation, due to issues like deep vein thrombosis (DVT), varicose veins, Raynaud's disease, etc.
- Venous stasis
- Cold agglutinin disease

You can simply do a lukewarm few seconds at the end of your shower, but the water temperature should remain above 60°F/15°C.

ant phase because we don't want you to get triggered and panic when you encounter the cold reality of the water.

Next time you take a shower, the last 30 seconds are going to be freezing cold. (If, like me, you're wimpy about the cold, unclench your jaw and drop your shoulders in anticipation. I totally feel you on this, but we can do this.) First, let's just imagine it. Take some slow breaths. Pretend there's a cold but gentle waterfall pouring down on you.

Keep breathing slowly as your body begins to acclimate to the cold. Sense the aliveness in your head, neck and shoulders, and down your arms.

When you actually try this in the shower, begin with the water warm. When you turn the water to cold (at whatever speed you prefer, slow or sudden is fine), try humming on the exhale as the cold hits you. It will get easier. Stay strong.

Over the next few weeks, at your own pace, gradually increase the amount of time you let the cold water run until you can tolerate it for three minutes. Once you can tolerate three minutes of cold water, you're ready for a ritual plunge.[4]

SUPPLIES

- Altar items to represent each element: Earth, Air, Fire, Water, Plastic, Metal, the Numinous, and DNA (an eyelash or a strand of hair is fine)[5]
- An altar cloth or tray to delineate sacred space
- A tub or body of cold water (between 50 to 60 degrees Fahrenheit or 10 to 15 degrees Celsius)
- A fresh clean towel for afterward

I. Create your altar, individually welcoming the Elements to help you carry this Dread. Pause here for a moment before you turn your attention to the water. Take time to sense how the supportive energies of the More Than Human affect your body and mind. Follow the path of the vagus nerve: How does your belly feel, your chest, your throat, your jaw, your forehead?

2. Focus your attention on slow rhythmic breathing. Notice where you carry Dread in your body. Place your hand there to bless your Dread—not to bless what's causing it, but the fact of its existence and its location in your body right now.

3. When you're ready, into the water you go, completely immersing yourself, even your head for a quick second if you can. Give yourself a minute to stabilize yourself. Remember to hum if that helps. Stay in the water for three to five minutes if you can.

4. When you come out of the water and towel off, take a moment to touch the place where your Dread was. Has it changed? How do you feel in relation to your Dread now? Acknowledge your courage. Thank your allies. Face the day.

Author's Notes

1   Berns, G. S., Chappelow, J., Cekic, M., Zink, C. F., Pagnoni, G., and Martin-Skurski, M. E. "Neurobiological Substrates of Dread." *Science* 312, no. 5774 (2006): 754–58. DOI: 10.1126/science.1123721.
2   Sadly, it looks like the rumored connection between sugar and Alzheimer's, dementia, and stroke is true: Miao, H., Chen, K., Yan, X., and Chen, F. "Sugar in Beverage and the Risk of Incident Dementia, Alzheimer's Disease and Stroke: A Prospective Cohort Study."

Journal of Prevention of Alzheimer's Disease 8, no. 2 (2021): 188–93. DOI: 10.14283/jpad.2020.62.

3   Slovic, Paul, and Weber, Elke U. "Perception of Risk Posed by Extreme Events." Columbia University and Wissenschaftskolleg zu Berlin, 2002. Accessed January 17, 2024. https://www.ldeo.columbia.edu/chrr/documents/meetings/roundtable/white_papers/slovic_wp.pdf.

4   The initial cold shock response of getting into the water can accelerate the sympathetic nervous system (the fight/flight response), whereas immersion of the head and face activates the parasympathetic branch of the nervous system, which lowers the heart rate, regulates blood pressure, and is anti-inflammatory. Every optimal-living bro dude with a podcast swears by cold water immersion, but for our Ritual purposes I encourage you to focus less on optimizing, conquest, triumph, or mind-over-matter, and more on befriending Dread, remembering to resource yourself before you engage with stress, and savoring the calm you feel once out of the water.

5   If your cold plunge is in your own bathtub, create an altar in your bathroom. If it's at the ocean, lake, or river, you'll want to take care that your altar can be safely left unattended.

Fear

Calling in the Dark

This is one of the core rituals I teach when leading a wilderness quest. The Numinous Quest, as we call it, is a 12-day journey to the backcountry where participants spend four days learning a combination of ritual literacy and survival skills, followed by four days and nights solo with just a tarp, water, sleeping bag, and first aid kit, then a return to the lodge for four more days of witnessing and integration. The purpose is to have a meaningful spiritual encounter with nature and the Self.[1]

People often ask, *What exactly do you do out there by yourself for four days?* This. We do rituals that help us confront and deal with the intensity of life. Most of the rituals are quite gentle and nurturing, actually. They're designed to help people orient toward safeness, opportunity, security, and self-care, even when conditions are spartan. But some of the rituals, like this one, train us to stand strong and look squarely at life as if to say, *Try me.*

If you really want to challenge yourself, you can do this ritual on a solo camping trip. That would be pretty hardcore, though, and perhaps just totally impractical for your life. At home in your backyard, you can set this up by turning off as many exterior and interior lights as possible. To do it inside, simply sit alone in a quiet dark room.[2] If you have acute mental health issues, do not do this ritual unless and until you have cleared it with a licensed mental health professional.

TIMING
This ritual is done at night. It might be nice to schedule for a Full Moon to keep you company.

SUPPLIES
- If you're outside, make sure you have many layers on and something thick and soft to sit on so you're warm enough and comfortable
- A flashlight for safety
- Items to delineate sacred space

1. Call in some Competent Protectors and imagine them at a distance where you can look to them for rescue, if necessary, but otherwise won't be involved or in the way.

COMPETENT PROTECTORS

Even though we're befriending our Fear, we aren't going
into this ritual completely vulnerable. First, we'll call in
some Competent Protectors, allies from the human and
More-Than-Human realms who feel protective. You should
trust them. You should have an uncomplicated love for
them. This may rule out a lot of humans. Know that you are
not limited to Competent Protectors in human form.

Competent Protectors can be Animals, Plants,
Elements, even Landscapes. Choose not only sensitive,
nurturing allies but also dynamic action-oriented
ones that you believe would intervene in a dangerous
situation. Simply invite them as you would a friend for
tea, *If you're available, I'd love you to come be with me now. I
could really use your support.*

The usual crew I call in are Bruce Springsteen, Dolly
Parton, an ancient crone ancestor whose name I don't
know, a mama Grizzly, a Percheron stallion, and this really
awesome Boulder that resides on a Mountain I love.

2. Delineate sacred space, either by drawing or imagining a circle around you on the ground. In the wilderness, you can use rocks, sticks, and pinecones to draw it
   out. At home, use a blanket or a circle of sacred objects

like rocks, crystals, or talismans. Sit or lie down inside the circle. Take a few cleansing breaths to center and orient yourself. Become aware of your surroundings and your relationship to them. What becomes more noticeable in the dark?

3. Practice some basic safety measures before you really get started. Stretch your arms and legs to invite your whole body to be present with you. Open your eyes and scan for safeness. Say the word *No* out loud. Say, *I've had enough.* Stand up and walk outside the sacred circle. These are all things you can do if you ever feel unsafe or emotionally flooded during this ritual. It's good to practice in advance, just like a fire drill.

4. When you're ready, step back inside the circle and establish yourself comfortably. Declare to your Fear out loud, *I'm ready when you are.* Then wait. You may notice some nervousness, apprehension, or dysregulation stir in your body. Keep breathing. Keep inviting Fear to be present.

5. When you sense Fear has arrived with a shift of the energy, either in the room or in your body, ask them, *What do you want from me?*

    Trust me when I say that Fear can be vicious. Don't be surprised if without so much as a hello your Fear says,

I want you to feel worthless or some other wincingly mean-spirited thing. As my Irish friend says, *Fear is a right arsehole.*

Tell your Fear, *No. Try again.*

Your Fear might say, *I want you to be small . . . smaller and smaller until you disappear.*

You just say, *No. I will not. Try something else.*

This could go on a long time. Do not give in to Fear. Hold firm against the meanness.

Fear: *I want you to suffer.*

You: *Absolutely not. What else?*

Fear: *I want you to be alone and outcast.*

You: *Fuck you. Anything else?*

Fear: *I want you to feel embarrassed about your body.*

You: *Ha ha; no, you jerk.*

Keep going like this until there is something reasonable that your Fear wants. Perhaps your Fear wants you to feel guilty about all the times you've put work before your health or friends or family. Fear of rejection could be a reasonable consequence of neglecting a relationship. For this, we ought to give Fear its due.

6. Ask Fear what it would accept as respectful acknowledgment of the role it plays in keeping you safe and in alignment with your values. You might say, *Okay, Fear . . . I will prioritize my loved ones ahead of work in the following ways: I will make a standing calendar appointment*

STANDING UP TO YOUR FEAR

After I signed the contract for my first book, I spent several months frozen with Fear, unable to write. I did the Calling in the Dark ritual. My Fear said it wanted me to die of humiliation. It wanted me to be pilloried on social media. It wanted me to feel stupid.

Naturally, this was unworkable. But I agreed to hire a sensitivity reader to look at my manuscript to make sure there was nothing in there deserving of repudiation or that might hurt people. I vowed to stay firm with my editor about keeping parts that felt important in terms of moving social justice forward. I committed to more sessions with my therapist to dig into the roots of self-confidence dependent on outward success and other people's evaluation of me. I promised to invite Fear to a vigil once a month where I would grieve for all the unwelcome parts of me that never found belonging in my family of origin, and for all the things I've done that I'm ashamed of. For half an hour once a month, I would acknowledge that my Fear came from a reasonable place and let myself feel afraid of being cast out of my social community.

In exchange, I asked my Fear to shut the fuck up and let me write the rest of the time.

And here we are, book number two! Written swiftly and with ease. No Fear.

for myself to send a hello text once a week. I will mark my cal-
endar with the birthdays, wedding anniversaries, and death
dates of my loved ones' loved ones, and I'll make sure to reach
out on or before those times. I will reward myself every time I
set a boundary at work in favor of my relationships.

7. Now begins the negotiation. Ask Fear for what you
   want in return. What boundary do you need to assert
   with your Fear around this issue?

8. Once you've arrived at a fair deal, you'll probably
   notice Fear just dissipates or slithers away. If not,
   simply dismiss your Fear now. Take a few cleansing
   breaths. Emphasize the exhales. Open your eyes and
   step out of the sacred circle or imagine it disappear-

ONE CAVEAT

Don't promise anything you can't give. You cannot cheat
the devil, and Fear can be a real shit sometimes. If you
don't respect Fear, it comes back worse. Do not disrespect
your Fear by making promises you won't keep.

Keep things simple, doable, and sincere. Most important,
don't give anything to Fear without getting something of
value in return. It's a fair negotiation or no deal.

ing around you. Declare the ritual over by saying out loud, *So be it. See to it.*[3]

AFTERCARE: Spend the next 30 to 60 minutes quietly nurturing yourself with a soothing drink, a bit of protein, some safe touch like wrapping yourself in a soft blanket, washing your face or moisturizing your skin, maybe put on some music or dab some essential oil on your wrist. Aftercare is especially important for this ritual. Think of something nourishing on the physical, emotional, mental, and spiritual level you can tap into now—big rituals call for more extensive aftercare.

Author's Notes

1   Thank you to Sparrow Hart for introducing me to this ritual on my first wilderness quest in Death Valley in 2007.
2   This ritual is rather robust and muscular, meant for when you really want to face your fears head on. Only do it when you're feeling strong. If you're feeling vulnerable, perhaps a gentler ritual would suffice. Consider the ritual for Confusion (which includes a segment on Fear) or Disquiet instead. Peruse the remedies for gentle support before diving headfirst into Fear. (Speaking of which, I sure hope you're not reading this book front to back in one sitting. If so, it's break time!)
3   Thank you to my dear friend Andrea Sexton-Dumas for modeling this way of affirming intentions and closing rituals.

Grief

Vigil

In the spring of 2012, I was invited to speak at a women's conference about accessing your intuition. I was new in the city, and when speaking to an audience that isn't well known to me, I tend to lead with some discussion around the social scorn that comes from publicly acknowledging our intuition. Because patriarchy derides and mocks women's intuition and spirituality, it's natural to feel a bit vulnerable and exposed even just attending a talk on intuition, and so I try to put people at ease right off the bat.

Later I attended the session of a fellow speaker, Shauna Janz, who spoke about Grief. At the time, Shauna was working as a grief counselor for families of victims of homicide, as well as leading grief groups for a nonprofit, supporting women recovering from intimate partner abuse. Back then, public acknowledgment of Grief was not nearly as common as it is today. I felt resonance with the topic and kinship with Shauna. We were both edgewalkers inviting strangers to take some intimacy risks—to engage in a deeper public

85

conversation about topics that are often shrouded in shame, taboo, and secrecy.

Today, it's not so difficult to find an expert in the specific type of Grief you're experiencing. Death doula Alua Arthur's TED Talk in 2023 has been viewed over a million times.[1] People of the Global Majority can find numerous therapists and organizations on social media offering Grief support around racialized experiences of bereavement, pregnancy loss, abuse in academia, spiritual harm, and more.[2] Members of the LGBTQIA2+ community exploring Grief during their second adolescence will find podcasts, articles, and forums.[3] Got climate Grief? Try the Good Grief Network website.[4] Is your neurodivergent Grief process plagued by autistic shutdowns?[5] Lived experience educators generously share their tips on TikTok. Do you feel ancestral Grief as a queer child-free person of northern European extraction? Shauna Janz is there for you.[6]

After attending one of Shauna's community Grief rituals in 2017, I was moved to make something similar a part of my ongoing spiritual practice. Over time, my practice evolved from a free-form sobfest in the Dark Moon phase, to a sturdier ritual container that feels better for my body and more secure for my broken heart.

Forgive me, but some sacred repetition is helpful here: Grief needs a strong container. Grief without a proper container is liable to ruin our relationships and our health, and echo through the generations. The two main containers we can use for Grief (or any intense emotions, for that matter) are Ritual and Community.[7] In the absence of those, Grief will use our body as the container. Unattended Grief can contribute to insomnia, heart disease, diabetes, inflammation, chronic pain, and a weakened immune system.

I now host a community Grief Vigil nearly every month online.[8] A Vigil is an ancient practice of sacred presence and devotion where we give full attention to our Grief. It provides a familiar structure and intentional space in which Grief can move freely.

What I've found after several years of setting aside a specific time to be with Grief is that it doesn't roam my mind or pop up unannounced the way it used to. Now it's as though my Grief has migrated to this regular date on the calendar where it sits like a pet dog eagerly awaiting its human. Where I used to be surprised by a wave of my Grief lurking just under the surface of awareness, I now find myself able to notice and feel Grief but hold it until I can provide the space and tenderness it needs to fully express. Sometimes I can arrive in the Vigil not feeling very much sadness, yet I still find the ritual to be calming and soothing.

Because Grief is still very much laced with social scrutiny, grieving communally is a radical act of resistance that connects us to our shared humanity. I strongly recommend you find fellow grievers to practice with you.

TIMING

To me, Grief rituals go well with Dark Moon energy, but anytime you need the ritual is the right time. Whenever you sense that collective Grief is welling up and spilling over into everyday interactions, or if people seem kinda snitty, short-tempered, or overwhelmed, a Grief Vigil is probably needed.

SUPPLIES

- An altar to grief that includes photos or written names of the Beloved Dead, supportive deities and amulets, and any offerings of food, drink, or incense that feel appropriate
- A poem to open and a poem to close[9]
- A candle and matches
- A 25-minute playlist of mellow or sad instrumental music

1. Either alone at your altar, or gathered with others, start by grounding through the breath—just three or four settling breaths to connect with the body.

2. Read the opening poem aloud.

3. Light the candle to signify the opening of sacred space. Begin the music.

4. Invite in the Beloved Dead by naming them out loud (or writing them in the chat if you're gathering

online). There are always the Unnameable Griefs, too—the names lost or concealed by displacement, enslavement, erasure, and secrecy. You can also name events, places you miss, regrets you carry, missed opportunities, errors of omission and commission, war, injustice, illness and disease, anything at all that brings you Grief.

5. You can either sit in quiet meditation, let yourself have a good cry, tend your altar, journal, or move to the music as you keep vigil for your grief.

6. When the music is finished, take a few moments to reconnect with your body and your breath. Stretch, twist, wiggle your fingers and toes, and look around the room at things that make you feel comforted and soothed. Make sure you feel grounded as you emerge from this ritual space.

7. Read the closing poem aloud. Blow out the candle. Shift to some grounding aftercare like having a snack, a shower, or going outside for a short walk around the block. You may or may not feel like having company, but I do recommend that you leave your grief on the altar for a little while and orient toward the present moment with the living, either human or nonhuman.[10]

THINGS TO DO DURING YOUR VIGIL

I like to drop a pinch of salt into a chalice of water as I name the Griefs out loud. The salt represents tears. After several months of vigils, I will take the salty water down to the ocean and pour all the tears into the sea. Sometimes only the ocean is big enough to hold all the Grief. If you're not near the ocean, you can allow the water to evaporate over several weeks, then harvest the salt again for your next Vigil.

Sometimes I write a list under the title "Things I Am Grieving Now." Sometimes I read poetry or prose about Grief and Loss. Some people like to burn their journal pages as part of the ritual, others dance with their Grief to move it through their body. Whatever you're inspired to do is perfect.

Author's Notes

1   Alua Arthur. "Why thinking about death helps you live a better life." TED, accessed January 20, 2024. https://www.ted.com/talks/alua_arthur_why_thinking_about_death_helps_you_live_a_better_life?language=en.

2   Instagram account "bipocdeathgrieftalk" (@bipocdeathgrieftalk). Accessed January 25, 2024. https://www.instagram.com/bipocdeathgrieftalk/.

3   Cohen, Adam James. "The Second Adolescence of LGBTQ+ Adult-

hood." *Psychology Today*, accessed January 19, 2024, https://www
.psychologytoday.com/ca/blog/second-adolescence/202305/the
-second-adolescence-of-lgbtq-adulthood.

4 Good Grief Network. "10 Steps to Resilience & Empowerment in a
Chaotic Climate." https://www.goodgriefnetwork.org/.

5 Fisher, Karla. "Autistic Grief Is Not Like Neurotypical Grief,"
Thinking Person's Guide to Autism, accessed January 9, 2024,
https://thinkingautismguide.com/2012/08/autistic-grief-is-not
-like-neurotypical.html.

6 Listen to our conversation about this: "Shauna Janz on Ancestral
Veneration in Child-Free and Queer Lineages," *The Numinous
Podcast*. Accessed November 25, 2023. https://crspagnola.podbean
.com/e/tnp212-shauna-janz-on-ancestral-veneration-in-child-free
-and-queer-lineages/.

7 I strongly recommend the work of Francis Weller as a framework
for living with grief individually and communally. Weller, Francis.
The Wild Edge of Sorrow: Rituals of Renewal and the Sacred Work of Grief.
North Atlantic Books, 2015.

8 The format of this ritual was cocreated with Holly Truhlar, a grief
therapist, facilitator, and community builder (www.hollytruhlar
.com), and Desiree Elizabeth Coutinho, a queer woman of color
therapist and clinical social work associate.

9 Though we may totally understand we're grieving, it can be sur-
prising just how defended the body can be against feeling it. Poetry
sets the stage for this ritual because it stimulates the sensing, emo-
tive parts of our brain. It has been described by poet, David Whyte,
as "the language against which we have no defence." Poetry for rituals of grief:

   Arthur Riley, Cole. *Black Liturgies: Prayers, Poems, and Medita-
tions for Staying Human*. Crown Publishing Group, 2024.

   Erfan King, Taraneh. *Conscious Grieving: The Path of Awakening
Through Loss*. Mind on Spirit Press, 2021.

   O'Donohue, John. *To Bless the Space Between Us: A Book of Blessings*. Crown Publishing Group, 2008.

Richardson, Jan. *The Cure for Sorrow: A Book of Blessings for Times of Grief.* Wanton Gospeller Press, 2020.

Translating, Franklin, and Fadwa Tuqan. n.d. "Despite the Great Distance, Existence Unites the Two: Translating the Poetry of Fadwa Tuqan." Accessed April 11, 2024. https://www.swarthmore.edu/sites/default/files/assets/documents/linguistics/2012_Huntington.pdf.

10 Nonhuman kin you could hang out with include houseplants, pets, trees, birds, clouds, or the Moon.

Loss

Funeral for a Void

This ritual is for ambiguous Loss, the kind without a death, yet marked by absence. It's for the type of Loss for which there are no sympathy cards, no trite condolences, no socially sanctioned gatherings or paid time off. Ambiguous Loss is the pain of someone leaving forever without saying goodbye. It's friendship breakups and parental estrangement. It's living with chronic illness that forces you out of a job. It's a loss of identity and social network upon retirement. It's caring for a loved one with Alzheimer's disease. It's the loss of language and cultural traditions due to immigration, displacement, or oppression. It's the grief of things that never happened that ought to have happened for you—presence instead of neglect, celebration instead of criticism, connection instead of isolation. This ritual is about creating a container for your disenfranchised grief and the innumerable Losses you suffer that receive no recognition.

There may be aspects of this Loss you feel ready to release, some not so much. Some parts you probably never will or can set free, and that's okay. That's just life. It's not black or white.

For this ritual, find objects to represent whatever you do wish to finally let go of; these will become grave goods to be buried during the ritual. Please be considerate of the environment and bury only things that will biodegrade and not leech toxic contaminants into the soil. No plastic, glitter, or polyester ribbon, for instance.

TIMING
As soon as you realize you're grieving.

SUPPLIES

- A piece of land you can dig in
- A playlist of funeral music for your Loss
- A candle and matches
- A handful of straw, raffia, dried grasses, or shredded paper
- A piece of pure cotton or linen fabric, about 10 by 10 inches
- Cotton or jute twine
- A small trowel or a shovel to dig
- Small offerings to your Loss such as flowers, food, drink, or incense
- Any grave goods that you would like to bury with this Loss

1. Choose the digging site in an area that gets enough moisture to break down the straw, fabric, and grave goods within a few months. Start the music and light a candle. You may wish to open sacred space by saying a few words about your Loss, how it has impacted you, and why now is the right time to bury it.

2. Take the straw and shape it into a small body on the piece of fabric. With each handful of straw, say all you want to say to your Loss before you say goodbye.

3. Wrap the fabric around the straw and tie it into a bundle with twine. Tie some twine where the neck, waist, and feet would be.

4. Dig a small hole in the rich earth. Dig it deep enough that it won't be found by an animal or gardener.

5. Make a bed of flowers for your Loss in the tiny grave. Place your Loss in the grave and position the grave goods on top. Speak from the heart about your Loss. Commit your Loss to the earth, calling upon the Greater Benevolent Powers to receive this Loss and keep it in their care. Cover your Loss with earth. If you like, you can leave a marker on top like a large rock or crystal, or you can plant a flower that blooms at a meaningful time, so you are inspired to remember this Loss and how it shaped you.

Overwhelm

Plant Medicine Steam

When you're overwhelmed, it's hard to drop everything and do a ritual. Usually there are very real factors contributing to your Overwhelm—time pressure, workload, major or multiple life changes, relational conflict, sleep problems, and living in late-stage racialized capitalism. These things are not alleviated by moon baths and aromatherapy. If you have deeply ingrained coping strategies that perpetuate Overwhelm, such as perfectionism, appeasement, and people pleasing, they make it even harder to break the cycle. If your nervous system is chronically overwhelmed, you will eventually hit a breaking point. I pray you'll do this ritual well before the utter meltdown stage.

For this ritual, we'll enlist our Plant allies to help with the physical, emotional, mental, and spiritual dimensions of Overwhelm. Trust that your body, heart, mind, and soul will be drawn to the perfect spiritual medicines for you. Don't worry too much about having extensive knowledge

SIGNS OF OVERWHELM

How do you know if you're becoming overwhelmed?
Usually a bunch of symptoms will start to pile up.
Headaches, elevated heart rate, poor sleep, low energy,
zoning out, lack of appetite, forgetting things, breakthrough
crying over seemingly small triggers, irritability, trouble
completing a thought, busy mind, clumsiness, and social
withdrawal are warning signs when clustered together or
dragging on for a long time.

of herbalism—these will not be ingested. Stick with plants
you know a bit about and really like.[1] Avoid
anything you're allergic to or unsure about.

TIMING
Ideally right before bedtime.

SUPPLIES
- A large bowl of very hot, steaming water
- Journal and pen or pencil
- A selection of herbs or essential oils (a small sprig or
  a few drops), one for each level: physical, emotional,
  mental, and spiritual
- A large towel

SOURCING

I suggest working with plants that are commonly found at a flower shop, garden center, or grocery store. The tea aisle is an interesting place to look for spellcraft ingredients. Yay for you if you're lucky enough to have a witch apothecary garden for less common herbs. Essential oils are also excellent, since fragrance acts directly on the olfactory bulb in the forebrain and influences emotional regulation.

1. Sit at a table with your bowl of steaming water and your plant allies in front of you.

2. Close your eyes for a moment to ground yourself. Wait until you detect a change in your body—a sigh, a yawn, a settling breath, watering eyes or mouth, tummy rumbling . . . these are all signs of your body relaxing.

3. Speak directly to the Cosmos and ask for help. If words don't come easily to you, you can simply say:

Great Mystery, I'm open to your physical support.

Add the physical support plant to the water and repeat the request:

I am open to your emotional support.

Add the emotional support plant to the water, and so on.

4. Once all the plants are in the water, drape the towel over your head and lean over the herbal steam bowl for a minute or two, breathing in support. Imagine taking in the spiritual medicine and support of the plants. With each breath, imagine that the support is distributed to every cell of your body. Rest here for as long as you like, breathing with the plants.

5. When you feel complete, lean back, remove the towel, and open your eyes. Slowly stand up and walk forward, looking forward, moving in a clockwise direction around the table or your chair. As you slowly walk in the circle, affirm out loud,[2]

I will not be whelmed.

Walk again around the circle saying,

I can say no to what I want to say no to.

Walk a third time around the circle saying,

I can say yes to what I want to say yes to.

Move instinctually now. That could mean you sit back down or even lie down to rest. It could mean you stretch or keep moving around, taking up more and more space in the room. Perhaps you continue to make declarative statements to affirm your power and agency:

I am sovereign.
My needs are important.
I am enough.

PLANTS FOR EACH LEVEL

Physical support: lavender, chamomile, nettles, milky oats

Emotional support: saffron, lemon balm, orange, rose, jasmine, lily, St. John's wort

Mental support: rosemary, sage, mint, North American skullcap

Spiritual support: bay leaf, dandelion, thyme, juniper, tulsi (holy basil), mugwort

---

6. When you sense the energy winding down, take the bowl to the sink and dump out the water as you thank the Cosmos for hearing you. Thank the plants for their support as you dispose of them. Bind this ritual by saying out loud, *And so it is.*

Author's Notes

1   Sowndhararajan, K., and Kim, S. "Influence of Fragrances on Human Psychophysiological Activity: With Special Reference to Human Electroencephalographic Response." *Scientia Pharmaceutica* 84, no. 4 (2016): 724–51. DOI: 10.3390/scipharm84040724.

2   If standing feels like too much right now, either do this in your mind or draw circles on your palm instead of walking in a circle.

    Thanks to Patti Elledge for this language: *I can say no to what I want to say no to. I can say yes to what I want to say yes to.*

Predicament

Burn the Good Candle

The problem with apocalypse is that it's not a problem, it's a Predicament. A problem has a solution, but in a Predicament we can only respond. A perennial Predicament is the notion that everyone you love will change, grow old, and die. To enjoy the richness of life that comes with love, you will necessarily suffer the agonizing sorrow of loss. It's a dilemma. A paradox. A Predicament.

The following ritual unfolds over several hours, likely days, possibly weeks or months. The longer it unfolds, the more poignant the Predicament, the more potent the healing. During this time, you'll take mental snapshots of fleeting moments. As you do this, you'll companion yourself through all the feelings that come with living bound to Predicament.[1] At the end of the ritual, you'll have created the only known corrective for the unpleasantness of perpetual quandary: experience and memory.

TIMING

Start this ritual on a memorable day such as a birthday, anniversary of an important event or the death of a loved one, or an astrologically significant time like Samhain, winter solstice, Beltane, or midsummer.[2]

SUPPLIES

- A metal skewer or sharp chopstick
- A beautiful beeswax candle, fancier than you'd normally buy

1. Call to mind the Predicament you find yourself in. It could be anything from the sweet poignance of love to the tragedy of large-scale collapse.

2. Using the skewer, carve a sigil or words on the candle that describe the Predicament. (If you'd prefer to keep this hidden, carve them on the bottom of the candle.)

3. Whenever you light the candle, meditate on your Predicament for a few moments then go about your regular activities. The candle is your witness and record of all the life you lived while tethered to this Predicament.

   The candle might be lit at the dinner table for special gatherings, or at your bedside when you're sick.

SIGIL WITCHERY

Sometimes a sigil is best, especially if you have a small candle. A sigil is a sign with magical properties.[3] To design your own sigil:

- Brainstorm five or six possible symbols related to your predicament
- Draw them in their simplest forms
- Layer them on top of each other

Here is a Sigil to Call in Support During Episodic Disability Due to Invisible Illness. I've used a spoon,[4] a ghost, a supportive container, love and compassion as my symbols, simplified them, and layered them into one image.

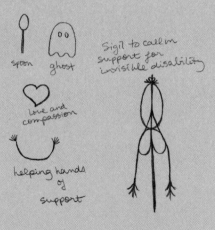

spoon

ghost

Sigil to call in support for invisible disability

love and compassion

helping hands of support

Light it when you receive good news and bad news. As you partner with the candle to be attentive to Predicament, the candle will slowly disappear. You'll need to work hard to keep up your end of the work, which is to pay attention to your emotions, sensations, and thoughts, and record them in your mind as memories.

4. If you can, try to be there for the candle when it finally extinguishes itself. As it expires, replay in your mind all the times you spent in its glow. Feel how the memories warm your insides, or how the fading light offers you relief and a sense of completion. Thank the light as you welcome the dark.

Author's Notes

1   If you want a clear end time for this ritual, say you want to complete it within a week, choose a small tealight candle that will burn for just 3 to 5 hours. If you're open to continuing for a season, a beeswax votive candle will burn 8 to 10 hours. To make this a year-long ritual to record all the highlights, invest in a 3-inch pillar that will burn over 30 hours. Remember that the first burn is always the most important—trim the wick to ¼ inch and allow it to burn until the entire top of the candle has a pool of liquified wax. Always burn your candle long enough for the wax to pool in an even layer on top, usually an hour per inch diameter.

2   Samhain: October 31. Beltane: May 1.

3   Zakroff, Laura Tempest. *Sigil Witchery: A Witch's Guide to Crafting Magick Symbols*. Llewellyn Worldwide, Limited, 2018.

4   This comes from spoon theory, an idea developed by blogger Christine Miserandino in 2003 to describe living with lupus. The concept spread through the disability community to the nondisabled community, and is now commonly used to describe living with chronic illness, invisible disability (including neurodivergence and emotional impairments), and episodic disability. If someone identifies as a "spoonie," it's a signal to be conscious of ableist assumptions, expectations, and demands placed upon them by a society governed by capitalism (and all the other isms). Miserandino, Christine. "The Spoon Theory." ButYouDontLookSick.com. Accessed September 15, 2023. https://butyoudontlooksick.com/articles/written-by-christine/the-spoon-theory/.

Rage

*Anger Ancestors and
Rage Role Models*

My fear of anger taught me nothing.
—Audre Lorde

Turbulent times are both a cause and effect of marginaliza-tion and trauma, and the two travel together. People already on the receiving end of prejudice and bias tend to be targeted even more as systems of power become destabilized. Rage is the proper response to inequity, injustice, and abuse of power.

Let's be clear about the kind of emotion I'm getting at here: The Rage I'm referring to is not the same as violence, intimi-dation, or meanness. I'm not talking about irascibility—being short-tempered—or bitterness, either. I'm talking about the explosive fury that comes from not having control over your circumstances, from a lack of agency, and from being silenced. This ritual is for the Rage born of injustice.

It can be hard for some people to make contact with their

Rage, even what they might consider "justified" anger or "holy outrage," because their associations with anger are connected to unhealthy models. Rage can feel really dangerous because it is so often coupled with the threat or enactment of violence. Memories can rush in and take over, confusing the sensations and clouding anger with fear. For those whose main experiences of Rage have been on the receiving end of abuse, feeling into this ritual might be fraught at first. What becomes possible if you give your Rage a clear boundary and a solid container, and permission to teach you something about yourself and what really matters to you?[1]

Like most big feelings, Rage benefits from a fairly even mix of containment and release. By containment I mean a right-sized container that's big enough to hold the emotion. Rage especially likes to express itself through the voice and arms. A ritual for Rage will need some strong boundaries and a clear space in which you can move and express without hurting or scaring yourself or someone else.

Let's begin by introducing as much safeness, support, and protection into the mix as possible. I invite you to think of some Rage Role Models. Invoke some powerful Anger Ancestors and Fierce Deities who carried their rage in a way that feels potent for you, like Medusa, Lilith, Durga, Baba Yaga, Sekhmet, and Inanna. Call upon Lyssa, the Greek goddess of mad rage, and Pele, the goddess of fire and wrath. Feel their energy around and within you.

Take out a piece of paper and make a list of historic figures who've expressed righteous anger in courageous, bold, bodily, vocal ways. I immediately think of Malcolm X, Nina Simone, Nawal El Saadawi, Fadwa Tuqan, Sojourner Truth, Flo Kennedy, Bella Abzug, Marsha P. Johnson, Sylvia Rivera, Stormé DeLarverie, and Andrea Dworkin. . . . Who else can you think of?

Then think of living legends who leverage their fury and resistance for collective good. List public figures such as Maxine Waters, Arundhati Roy, Sahar Khalifeh, Riki Wilchins, and Alexandria Ocasio-Cortez, or entertainers such as Amanda Seales, Samantha Bee, Ali Wong, and Michelle Wolf.[2] Which names come to you now? Write down all the resonant bands, musicians, and rappers you can think of whose lyrics speak your mind.

Then add all the fictional characters whose expressions of Rage incite a spark of excitement in you. Remember Angela Bassett's character made meme-famous, Bernadine Harris, in the movie *Waiting to Exhale,* cooly walking away from her soon-to-be-ex-husband's exploding car? Like that. Now we're talkin'.

Then, as a physical warm-up to your ritual for Rage, put on a raucous song and turn it up loud. Anger loves to discharge through the arms, legs, and throat. For the length of one song, use your whole body to amplify your Rage.[3] Yell every swear word you know! Punch the air! If that feels more violent than you like, and you are in really good physical shape and don't have a back problem or bad knees,

IMPORTANT CONSIDERATIONS
FOR RAGE ROLE MODELS

For those of us who are non-Black, it's important to name that the racial stereotype of the "angry Black woman" is a well-worn trope used to discredit Black women's holy outrage and resistance to oppression. They are unjustly patronized and dismissed as irrational, overbearing, and ill-mannered. Black women's safety—their very lives—are threatened for the slightest expression of anger. The anger of white women, even under patriarchy, is still much more acceptable in a culture governed by white supremacy than the anger of People of the Global Majority. Especially if you're white, be aware of this as you source energy from iconic Rage Role Models.

Though I've named icons from many cultural backgrounds, not all of them are meant for every reader. As with all spiritual practices, I recommend you tap into your own cultural and communal lineages before you invoke the Ancestors of others. You can praise those icons by studying them. Say their names, credit them, amplify their message. But be discerning with regard to intimacy with them—think twice before claiming the Ancestors of others for spiritual succor. If you're not sure whether they should go on your altar or not, consider opting for not. Instead, include them in your prayers, and thank them for their example rather than ask them for intercession.

instead you can lift heavy shit![4] Do bicep curls with a sack of potatoes. Do deadlifts with a small child.[5] Do squats with a box of printer paper. Lifting heavy things releases endorphins, increases confidence, and makes us feel powerful.

Do these things to strengthen the energetic container for your ritual for Rage, then proceed with your ritual.

TIMING

Do this ritual when:

- You feel pent-up pressure inside
- You notice you're looping in heated arguments in your head
- Your righteous anger at the world is starting to spill over into your relationships
- You've done all the grief rituals but the dysregulation is still there—maybe you're not sad, you're mad

SUPPLIES

- Pen and paper bags
- Several glasses and jars from the recycling bin or thrift shop

1. Identify all the things igniting your holy outrage right now and write them down on individual paper bags.

2. Put a piece of glassware in each paper bag.

3. SMASH THEM.

Author's Notes

1   Audre Lorde, "The Uses of Anger: Women Respond to Racism,"
    https://www.blackpast.org/african-american-history/speeches
    -african-american-history/1981-audre-lorde-uses-anger-women
    -responding-racism.

2   There's always a risk when elevating living people that you'll live
    long enough to see your heroes disappoint you. Consider this para-
    graph a spell, that our Rage Role Models always remain tethered
    to our shared values, and when they drift, may the Greater Powers
    call them in.

3   If you prefer more of an intellectual exploration of Rage before
    you get physical, see below starting with Audre Lorde's essay, "The
    Uses of Anger: Women Responding to Racism," found in the book:
    Lorde, Audre. *Sister Outsider: Essays and Speeches.* Clarkson Potter/
    Ten Speed, 2012.

    Traister, Rebecca. *Good and Mad: The Revolutionary Power of
    Women's Anger.* Simon & Schuster/Marysue Rucci Books, 2018.

    Chemaly, Soraya. *Rage Becomes Her: The Power of Women's Anger.*
    Atria Books, 2019.

    Lee, Lela. "Angry Little Asian Girl: Moments with My Mother."
    AngryLittleGirls.com. Accessed September 12, 2023. https://angry
    littlegirls.com/products/angry-little-asian-girl-moments-with-my
    -mother?pr_prod_strat=copurchase&pr_rec_id=6d9398eb0&pr_rec
    _pid=7612991111385&pr_ref_pid=8154640548057&pr_seq=uniform.

4   "Lift Heavy Shit." Workouts by Sims, Stacy T. Workouts found on
    YouTube.

5   Sims, Stacy T., and Yeager, Selene. *Next Level: Your Guide to Kicking
    Ass, Feeling Great, and Crushing Goals Through Menopause and Beyond.*
    Harmony/Rodale, 2022.

6   Don't drop the child or they will be mad at you! Also, if you have
    roommates or live with family, it's probably best to do this ritual
    while you have the house to yourself. If there are kids in the house,
    this could be really confusing for them if you don't explain it to

them. Depending on the nature of your child, this could be a good way to teach them about safe, controlled discharge of anger. Make sure you walk them through the entire process and explain the ritual step-by-step—skipping right to smashing could send mixed messages.

Stagnation

Shake It Out

This ritual is for times when you feel stuck, constrained, confined, trapped, pressured to stay small, or silenced.

Stagnation and stuckness can feel like pressure. It can make your breathing shallow, your spine stiffen, or your body sweat. Some people feel it as a desire to push or run away. Some folks would rather curl up into a ball and disappear. There can be a low-grade panicky feeling that persists no matter how much you try to relax or distract yourself. You may find yourself engaging in constant scanning behaviors like endless daydreaming or scrolling online looking for other lives you could live, relationships you could be in, jobs you could apply for, training you could take, places you could live. Anywhere but here, anything but this.

When options are too many or too few and you're immobilized by indecision, that's the time to partner with the Greater Powers.

For this ritual, you'll need a noisemaker. It could be a

glass jar with some beans in it, or a carton of Kraft macaroni. It really doesn't matter what it is. The key thing is that ultimately you're going to empty your noisemaker, so it should be something you can open and empty with ease. (Not a sacred rattle made of rawhide, for instance.) You're going to make some noise, so you'll probably want a measure of privacy.

TIMING
You may want to schedule this ritual for a Monday or a Wednesday.[1]

SUPPLIES
- A candle
- A loud rattle—jelly beans in a jar or a box of macaroni, or similar
- A song that makes you want to belt it out loud—mine is "Shake It Out" by Florence and the Machine
- A receptacle to catch the contents of your noisemaker such as a tea towel, a bowl

1. Light your candle to open sacred space. Sit with your noisemaker in hand and simply notice your breath. Get a baseline of how you're feeling. Don't linger in the sensation of stuckness, just notice for a second or two how it's held in your body.

PLANETARY MAGIC

Monday is ruled by the Moon and the Moon is all about change. The Moon is Queen of This Too Shall Pass. If you want immediate manifestation, she's your gal. If you want a new thing to come into your life to shake things up, consider doing this ritual on a New Moon. If you're ready for something to be washed away and moved along, time your ritual for a Full Moon, the time of culmination.

Wednesdays are ruled by Mercury, a fast-moving planet. Mercury is the opposite of stagnation. When working with Mercury, change comes with speed. They're about conveyance, delivering you from one place to another. Maybe not the best for long-term planning, but for a speedy redirect? Mercury is a good bet.

2. Begin to shake your noisemaker, slowly, and just listen to the sound in the air. Imagine the sound waves parting the air and moving the energy around. Keep breathing as you shake your noisemaker, parting the air with sound waves, for a full minute.

3. When your arm is tired of shaking, stop. Listen to the silence. Let your breath and the energy settle for

a moment. How does the sound, herald of movement, make you feel?

4. Get a little more unstuck by slowly moving to a standing position.[2] As you get up, focus on the soles of your feet, sensing the solid ground. Press play on your Belt It Out song. Turn it up. Start shaking your noisemaker to the beat. You might move both arms in a shaking motion to really bring that shake it off / shake it out / get unstuck kind of energy to your upper body. Give your body and voice and noisemaker the freedom to do what they need to do. Be part of the sound; make your own waves. Give it your all!

5. When the song ends, open your noisemaker and let the insides spill out. Scatter the beans on the fabric or dump the jellybeans into your mouth or pour the macaroni into a pot to cook up later. What do you experience watching the contents move from containment to liberty? What do you notice in your gut, your chest, your jaw, your eyes, when you see and feel the release?

Some people want to laugh or be playful; some feel a bit tearful; some are worried about waste—scan for the best feeling you can find and go with it. Give yourself a few minutes, maybe the length of another

song or a replay of your Belt It Out track, to enjoy a
sense of freedom and welcome disruption.

6. Come back into quiet stillness in front of your candle.
   What do you notice with sensation and emotion now?
   What do your face, skin, torso, and legs feel like? Scan
   for the best sensation or thought you can find and linger there a moment. Give thanks to any planet, deity,
   or guide who supported you today (musical artists
   included). Blow out your candle to close the ritual.

Author's Notes

1   The day of the week you select for your rituals can add another
    layer of potency to your magic. Mondays are ruled by the Moon,
    who presides over the body, so rituals having to do with health can
    be good on that day. Tuesday is ruled by Mars, who can help with
    initiative and motivation. Wednesday is ruled by Mercury, who is a
    great conveyer, moving everything from people to markets to mes-
    sages through the world; anything to do with travel, commerce,
    and communication is within this planet's purview. Jupiter rules
    Thursday and blesses us with increase, expansion, and spiritual
    growth. Friday is the day of Venus, planet of love and beauty, mag-
    netism and union, luxury, sensuality, and the arts. Saturday belongs
    to Saturn, known as Father Time and Lord of the Harvest, who
    helps assert boundaries. Sunday is ruled by the Sun and supports
    constancy, centeredness, visibility, and a strong sense of self. To give
    your rituals even more of a boost, consult www.planetaryhours
    .net and perform your spell during the hour that corresponds to

the planet you'd like to enlist for help. To learn more about Astro-
Magic and planetary propitiation to enhance your rituals, see the
AstroMagic miniseries on The Numinous Podcast, episodes 198—
204, starting with the center of it all, the Sun: Spagnola, Carmen.
"TNP198: AstroMagic Miniseries with Eliza Robertson and The
Sun." *The Numinous Podcast*. Podcast audio, July 2, 2023. Accessed
February 25, 2024. https://crspagnola.podbean.com/e/tnp198-astro
-magic-miniseries-with-eliza-robertson-and-the-sun/.

2   You can definitely do this ritual sitting or lying down—use whatever movement is available to you. If standing is available to you,
you'll have the added benefit of physically shifting to sympathetic
nervous system dominance, which is how we harness energy, stim-
ulation, and provoke motivation. The aim is to use sound to inspire
some motion to counteract Stagnation. If standing isn't for you,
notice if your upper body has the urge to reach or stretch. Follow
that impulse!

PART III

Remedies

Acknowledgment · 123 ✦ Appreciation · 134

Awe · 140 ✦ Balance · 146

Celebration · 151 ✦ Connection · 156

Conservation · 161 ✦ Movement · 165

Nurturance · 169 ✦ Pronking · 174

Protection · 178 ✦ Renewal · 185

Wholeness · 188

Acknowledgment

Dignity Circle

My life was set upon a completely new path when I attended the Canadian government's Truth and Reconciliation Commission (TRC) public testimonies of residential school survivors in 2012. Prior to that, I had cursory knowledge of residential schools through books, documentaries, and personal friends who were survivors. But the ritual of bearing witness alongside hundreds of others in a large and fully packed auditorium, listening to survivors tell their stories in their own words, and hearing them ask for reparation measures that felt fair to them, was a wholly transformative experience that altered my personality and how I move through the world.

The difference between knowledge and Acknowledgment is the dignity restored when suffering is truly heard and integrated at the heart level. Sometimes we cognitively understand that something terrible happened to us, or that we've caused harm, but our understanding remains surface-level or abstract until we become profoundly present with Acknowledgment and experience a deeper, felt-sense understanding.

Without sincere Acknowledgment, wounds fester, resentment and bitterness lay dormant, and relationships quietly deteriorate and eventually crumble, often for what seems on the surface to be a small provocation. Lack of Acknowledgment is one of the fatal flaws of a poor apology and often leads to an escalation of conflict instead of the hoped-for result. Any apology that begins with, *I'm sorry*

DIGNITY FOR ALL

Truth restores dignity to both victims and perpetrators. Because of my engagement with the Truth and Reconciliation Commission's mandate, I have more respect for myself as a white settler. I try harder to be honest with myself about my complicity in white supremacy. I'm more sincere in my efforts to integrate the TRC's 94 Calls to Action into my life.[1] When I do a Land Acknowledgment, the voices of Indigenous survivors echo in my heart. Land Acknowledgment is a ritual I do to transform my settler relationship to the Land from one shaped by capitalism and colonialism to one of stewardship and solidarity with my neighbors, both human and Other Than Human.

you feel . . . is getting off on the wrong foot. (In case it's not obvious, it's the "you" part that undermines the statement.)

Acknowledgment is about what I did, my part in the conflict, how I wounded another. If I'm the one asking for Acknowledgment, it's about how I was impacted and how I feel about that. A practice of frequent and heartfelt Acknowledgment is good medicine for the spiritual vitality of a relationship or community.

For some, Acknowledgment is difficult because it elicits shame. Occasionally an injured person will spend a great deal of time empathizing with the perpetrator of harm before they will touch the depths of their own pain or the extent of the harm they endured.

> *My partner was treated terribly by his father, so I understand how his trauma makes him act so poorly toward me and the kids.*

> *My mom has a mental illness—she did the best she could.*

> *My friend is neurodivergent and has suffered a lot in her life, so it makes sense that she doesn't always hear me and can be a bit punitive at times. It hurts but it's not her fault.*

> *My siblings and I don't apologize because we didn't grow up in a family culture of repair or taking responsibility for*

hurting each other's feelings. We just let it go and move on. Family is family, you know?

Of course we want to empathize with those who hurt us, but we don't need to de-center or diminish our own pain in order to do so.

As an ongoing life practice of owning your (very valid) need for Acknowledgment, start by asking for witnessing from safe-enough people. Try a therapist, a crisis line, or a friend removed from the situation who's a really good listener. If the topic feels too vulnerable to share with anyone, you can record yourself and then play it back to yourself, while assuming the stance of a loving and supportive wit-

SMALL "N" NARCISSISM

It's not always the case, but when dealing with folks who have narcissistic traits, there can be secondhand shame that lingers when a perpetrator refuses to acknowledge what they've done.[2] If the perpetrator doesn't have the capacity to feel shame, the victim will internalize it for them. You may need to accept that you'll never receive Acknowledgment from them or feel heard, but you don't have to feel shame about that. That's on them, not you. Their loss, my friend.

ness. When you speak, share your truth without qualifying it. In other words, simply take it as a given that the person who hurt you is good and worthy of love regardless of bad behavior, but/and/also, just for a moment, stop centering them. This is about you. Center yourself.

For this remedy, you'll state a boundary violation and ask someone for Acknowledgment.[3] We'll refer to this someone as the Listener. This roleplay can prepare you for a real-life conversation, or it can be a proxy in times when you know the Listener will never genuinely engage in discussion about what they did. It might help to gather your thoughts and write down what you want to say before you begin the ritual.[4]

To stay grounded, I suggest you set a timer for 10 minutes or less.[5] Remember: You're just a little mammal. Your nervous system can only take so much time immersed in stress before your prefrontal cortex will fizzle out. The timer creates a somatic and energetic boundary. If you're growing overwhelmed, confused, or vividly reliving the scene, stop sooner. Slower is better, less is more.

TIMING
Anytime.

SUPPLIES
- Two chairs

- Evergreen boughs
- Four candles and matches

1. Set your chairs in a circle of evergreen boughs.[6] Place the candles in a line between your chair and what will be the Listener's chair when you invite them in. Have your matches in hand. Sit in your chair and take a few settling breaths.

2. Imagine a wide circle of Compassionate Witnesses surrounding both you and the empty chair awaiting your guest. Feel the love and empathy, the understanding and strength of these Witnesses. Imagine yourself held in a large, strong circle of love.

TREE MAGIC

The evergreen boughs are for your spiritual protection. Cedar prepares the heart and cleanses the body and mind. Pine provides courage, fortitude, and long-lasting magic. Spruce denotes generosity and pure intentions. Fir conveys messages to other realms. Juniper spiritually purifies and cleanses space by banishing any dark or heavy energies.

3. Light the first candle to represent yourself and the inner flame of your resilience.

4. Light the second candle to represent the Listener.

    When you're ready, invite the Listener to enter the space and sit across from you in the other chair. How does their presence change the energy in the room and in your body? Take your time.

5. Light the third candle to represent your truth. State your needs and feelings as specifically as you can. Tell the Listener how you perceive what happened, how it impacted you, and how you feel about it. For example:

    I'm still really hurt by what you said. I feel like we moved to repair without any real Acknowledgment of how that impacted me. A genuine apology would help me feel more complete and trusting that we're truly on the same page.

6. Now light the final candle. Feel even more warmth and love from your Compassionate Witnesses. Sense them drawing nearer to you.

    Imagine the Compassionate Witnesses responding in the most appropriate way, meeting your need for affirmation:

    We hear you and we're so sorry. You exist and you mat-

ter. Your feelings matter. Your pain matters. You deserve love and care. You deserve to be heard. You deserve better. We're here. We're with you. We appreciate you. We support you. We love you.

7. When the energy shifts to wrapping up or the timer goes off, blow out the fourth candle. As the smoke wafts, the message from your Compassionate Witnesses permeates the air so that the molecules of air in the room are made up of their love and devotion to you.

8. Blow out the third candle and say aloud, *This is my testimony.* As the smoke rises, know that your truth has been received and affirmed by the Cosmos.

9. Dismiss the Listener, blow out their candle, and feel their presence diminish and leave the room.

10. Pause for a moment to sit with the first candle, the inner flame of your resilience. Bring the energy of that flame inside yourself. Where do you carry the glow of resilience inside of you?

    As you blow out the candle, know that your truth is conveyed by the smoke to the four corners of the Cosmos.

11. After you dismantle the ritual space, wash your hands of this. Slowly wash your hands with tenderness and care under warm running water. Wash your face, perhaps even your hair and your body. Put on fresh clothes. You are a new person with dignity restored, reconnected to your inherent worth, shining warrior of your own cause, advocate for your soul.

Author's Notes

1   The Truth and Reconciliation Commission of Canada was active from 2008 to 2015. According to Wikipedia, "It provided residential school survivors an opportunity to share their experiences during public and private meetings held across the country. The TRC emphasizes that it has a priority of displaying the impacts of the residential schools to the Canadians who have been kept in the dark from these matters."

Wikipedia contributors. "The Truth and Reconciliation Commission of Canada." Wikipedia, The Free Encyclopedia. Accessed February 6, 2023. en.wikipedia.org/wiki/Truth_and_Reconciliation _Commission_of_Canada#cite_note-link.galegroup.com-6.

Document "Calls to Action," Government of British Columbia. Accessed October 21, 2023. https://www2.gov.bc.ca/assets /gov/british-columbians-our-governments/indigenous-people/ aboriginal-peoples-documents/calls_to_action_english2.pdf.

Gray Smith, Monique. *Speaking Our Truth: A Journey of Reconciliation*. Orca Book Publishers, 2017.

2   This is small "n" narcissism to distinguish it from capital "N" narcissistic personality disorder (NPD). Narcissism is a trait related to having extremely high self-regard and a degree of entitlement or

self-absorption, whereas NPD is more than being inconsiderate or selfish. It's a spectrum and pattern of behavior noticeable quite early in life that involves exploitiveness, arrogance, constant need for excessive admiration, a lack of empathy, and preoccupation with an idealized and grandiose sense of self and success in both behavior and fantasy. Children display a healthy narcissism that hopefully develops into high self-esteem and intrinsic self-worth. Everyone is a bit narcissistic in the sense that we conceive of ourselves as the central figure in our own personal narrative, and sometimes we can have our blinders on and not be aware of our impact on others. Most people can receive that feedback, apologize, and try to do better from then on. But some people don't, won't, or can't, and sometimes that's because of an underlying mental health issue like NPD.

3   Do a dry run with a lesser hurt for this ritual, not your most devastating situation ever, and build some stamina for it first. Maybe rehearse this with your therapist. If what the Listener did was deeply traumatic, you may need (quite literally) years of therapy before this ritual feels possible. Pace yourself and if you start becoming flooded with emotion, stop immediately. Move to soothe—what gentle action would feel reassuring right now? Perhaps wrap yourself in a thick blanket, listen to calming music and hug yourself as you rock side to side, take a warm shower, or relax with a hot or cold drink. Remember principles of trauma-sensitive witchcraft: We're not going to diminish or push through signs of distress.

4   You can also do this ritual if you owe someone an apology and would like to lay a spiritual foundation first, or if they've set a no-contact boundary with you. Take care here to honor consent: Do not put words in their mouth, even in your imagination. Simply speak to them from the heart without expecting or asking for understanding or forgiveness. Trust in the Greater Powers to deliver your message to them somehow. Do not impose your will on them in your magic.

If you're the one offering Acknowledgment in this ritual, begin with self-regulation. Sit in the chair and take some settling breaths. Ground your sit bones and your feet. Lengthen your spine. Drop your shoulders. Even if you really hurt someone badly, you are still lovable and forgivable. Imagine the person you hurt seated in the other chair.

Fill in the blanks for the first four parts in the list that follows. All four parts are required for the apology to be complete, but there's still no guarantee it will be accepted. However, you'll have helped, at least partially, to restore dignity to the parties involved, which is the true medicine at the heart of Acknowledgment.

1. Acknowledge: *I'm sorry that I* . . . (repeat the specific thing, using the words the injured person used), *and that I hurt* (any and all of the people impacted). Light a candle.

2. Empathize: *It makes sense to me that you feel* . . . (repeat the feeling words they used or at least try to guess how they might feel). Light a candle.

3. Explain: *I was not tracking how this would impact you because* . . . (Explain what happened—not to justify but rather to explain how your behavior is not their fault or responsibility. For example, . . . *because I was so stressed out with work, but I know it's unfair to dump that on you.*) Light a candle.

4. Repair: *In the future, I will* . . . (Explain how you will undertake this new practice to change behavior or improve the situation.) Light a candle.

5. Once complete, blow out the candles one by one so the smoke can carry your message far and wide.

5   The prefrontal cortex is the region of the brain responsible for executive functioning including your ability to form words and coherent thoughts. As a trauma-sensitive practitioner, ten minutes is the maximum amount of time I'd want someone to try to function under stress.

6   If the other person you're imagining in this ritual is someone you want to stay close to, create a large circle of evergreen boughs around the two chairs. If instead you want to assert a boundary with this person, lay the evergreens in a line on the floor as a partition between you, or encircling your chair only. Take time when setting up the chairs and sense the correct distance between you. If proximity causes discomfort or anxiety, move the chairs farther apart until it's manageable.

Appreciation

Treasured Flower Friend

This Appreciation remedy is a great way to practice full and loving presence to what is in front of us. It helps us scan for the goodness around us and land a sense of safeness and connection in our body. With repetition of this remedy, it becomes easier to co-regulate with Plants, Animals, and even other humans fairly quickly. In apocalypse times, co-regulation is as important as clean air and water. If you ever find yourself utterly lacking in good-quality human contact, try co-regulating with the Other Than Human using this remedy as the framework.[1]

Spending time in the energy of Appreciation is a gateway to deeper communion with others, both human and More Than Human. For this remedy we'll partner with a flower, because it's so easy to appreciate their beauty. When we gaze upon a gorgeous bloom, our latent capacity for Appreciation unfurls as though we ourselves are the flower.[2]

While gratitude and Appreciation overlap, for our purposes let's delineate them a bit. Let's say that gratitude is expressing thankfulness for the benefit someone or something affords us, whereas Appreciation is acknowledging what they mean to us. In other words, Appreciation is about recognizing inherent worth and intrinsic qualities that stir a positive response in us. It's less about *thank* you for doing this or that for me, and more about *you* are so this, I love how *you* are that, it's so wonderful the way *you* . . .

When we commune with flowers through Appreciation, we connect ourselves to the web of life from which we came, to which we belong, and for which we are endowed with stewardship. A meaningful relationship with a plant community of any kind, whether a flower garden, vegetable patch, mossy forest, tidal wetland, or sagebrush grassland, re-embeds us in an ecosystem and strengthens our sense of belonging.

TIMING
Anytime.

SUPPLIES
- A glass of water
- A flower that you find especially wonderful

1. Read through the following grounding exercise to get the gist of it, or record yourself reading it. Before you approach the flower, close your eyes and take a few set-

tling breaths, really emphasizing the exhale. Begin the guided meditation:

Exhale your roots all the way through the soil and the bones of the Ancestors, the underground waters, right down to the fiery molten core of the Earth. Use the air of your breath to blow away any burdensome energies so they can be composted by the Earth.

Inhale, drawing up elemental goodness from the heart of the Earth, pulling up the warmth of the Earth's core, drawing in soothing medicines of the mineral-rich underground waters, the wisdom of the Ancestors, and the life-giving nutrients of the soil.

Feel this revitalizing energy traveling through you and upward, connecting with the Atmosphere, Clouds and Sun, and the Cosmos beyond. Feel your energy reaching up as though you are heliotropic, a flower extending themself upward from the soil to the heavens. Turn your palms up, resting your hands with palms up in your lap.

Receive the blessings of solar and celestial energies on your face and into your upturned palms. Absorb them into your own fiery core, allowing them to travel through all the layers of your own body. Let them land in you, and rest. Settle back into a relaxed position, open your eyes, and turn your attention to the flower.

Offer a bit of water to the flower as a greeting.

Some flowering plants, for instance cacti or succulents, may only want a few drops, whereas a cut flower will likely appreciate a whole glass of fresh water (and perhaps even a fresh cut at the base of its stem so it's easier for it to absorb the water offering).

2. Tune in to this flower and focus on what you appreciate about them. Notice at least 10 things you appreciate about them. What effect does this Appreciation have on your body?

3. Count the colors you can see on the flower from the stem all the way to the upper edges of the petals, including how the light and shadows alter your perception of the most prominent color, giving it several tones and hues. Note any pollen or dust on the surface of the plant. What emotions and sensations do the colors provoke?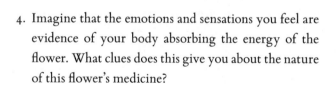

4. Imagine that the emotions and sensations you feel are evidence of your body absorbing the energy of the flower. What clues does this give you about the nature of this flower's medicine?

5. Spend a few moments breathing in rhythm with the flower. Inhale their special medicine. As you exhale and the carbon dioxide of your respiration is trans-

mitted through the air, imagine them receiving your medicine in return. Sense yourself in deeper communion, each appreciating the other. What do you treasure about them?

6. After you've practiced this remedy with a flower, try it with other subjects. Spend the next several days in active Appreciation practice with all kinds of plants and Earth elementals such as rocks, trees, and fungi, noticing all the meaningful relationships you can cultivate this way.

   Continue on to all the other elements including Water, Fire, Air, Metal, Plastic, DNA, and expressions of the Numinous. Eventually extend this to humans. Make this a lifelong practice.

Author's Notes

1 To survive four years in Nazi concentration camps, Viktor Frankl noted that "intensification of inner life" helped the prisoners to cope. He describes a poignant moment of sensing his wife in the form of a bird while digging a ditch. Frankl, Viktor E. *Man's Search for Meaning: Gift Edition*. Beacon Press, 2015.

2 This ritual is inspired by the work of Pam Montgomery who has written several books and teaches courses on plant spirit communication. Recommended resources for plant connection:

   Montgomery, Pam. *Plant Spirit Healing: A Guide to Working with Plant Consciousness*. Inner Traditions/Bear, 2008.

Geniusz, Mary Siisip. *Plants Have So Much to Give Us, All We Have to Do Is Ask: Anishinaabe Botanical Teachings*. University of Minnesota Press, 2015.

Kimmerer, Robin Wall, and Gray Smith, Monique. *Braiding Sweetgrass for Young Adults: Indigenous Wisdom, Scientific Knowledge, and the Teachings of Plants*. Lerner Publishing Group, 2022.

Charlie, Luschiim Arvid, and Turner, Nancy J. *Luschiim's Plants: Traditional Indigenous Foods, Materials and Medicines*. Harbour Publishing, 2021.

Prechtel, Martín. *The Unlikely Peace at Cuchumaquic: The Parallel Lives of People as Plants: Keeping the Seeds Alive*. North Atlantic Books, 2012.

Awe

Little Miracles Everywhere

Fascinating research has emerged in the study of emotions in the past 20 years around the special role of Awe in the human experience. At the Greater Good Science Center at the University of California, Berkeley, the psychology and neuroscience of well-being is studied.[1] Those at the center try to understand things like compassion, altruism, and happiness to see if their findings can have a positive influence on society and policy. What they've discovered about Awe could have a profound impact on social functioning both interpersonally and collectively, if we'd only let it. Awe supports collaborative, prosocial behaviors, a sense of interconnectedness, and a feeling of enfoldment into something bigger and more wonderful than mundane reality. Plus, it regulates our nervous system.

What *is* Awe, exactly?

Awe is usually caused by something vast, or beyond our normal perceptual framework and ability to comprehend. Think of an incredible vista seen from a high place. If you're lucky enough to have been to the Grand Canyon or to the top of the Eiffel Tower, or climbed to the peak of a mountain, you probably felt something within range of Awe. Large and sublime natural spaces and unfamiliar flora and fauna can trigger Awe. I've never seen a giant corpse flower or a thousand-year-old bodhi tree up close, but I bet they're awe-inspiring. I've been fortunate to grow up among giant cedar trees. Some are so large they require seven adults to reach around them, barely able to touch fingers, to envelope the trunk in a giant hug. Awe is an experience we can't easily reproduce—we can't just call up an aurora borealis or command a butterfly to alight on our finger or transplant a gigantic cedar to our backyard.

Incredible feats of human capacity can also induce Awe. Think about Cirque du Soleil, the Paralympics, masterworks of art and architecture, or giving birth. When the novelty wears off, the Awe tends to wane, as well. We're likely to be a lot more wide-eyed and excited about seeing a buffalo on the side of the road than a cow, aren't we?

No shade to cows! They are still exciting! But Awe is more than delight. Awe has a slack-jawed quality to it. You lose your breath for a second. You are momentarily frozen, suspended in rapt attention. The major difference between fear and Awe is the sense of safeness. Awe is a big feeling, but it doesn't completely overwhelm.

Instead, we feel enfolded into something bigger than ourselves, enveloped into a larger collective, gathered and connected. That, in turn, triggers our desire to collaborate—we want to be part of this, to transcend our smaller egoic self, our mundane human problems, our quibbles and quarrels, and actively participate in something beautiful and meaningful. We are connected to the specialness, uniqueness, and rarity of our own existence, and of our fellow travelers in this lifetime. Like, what are the chances we are all here on this rock hurtling through space and we get to experience sunrises and sunsets and . . . *space*? Awe induces an urge to be fully present and make the most of our lives, or at least this moment. Awe doesn't trigger social competition or the reciprocity problem the way love or friendship can. Awe makes us want to be and do better, regardless of whether we receive anything in return. Awe feels like a generous enoughness.

In the body, Awe stimulates the part of our nervous system responsible for social engagement. We're attuned and able to give our attention. We feel curiosity, inspiration, the desire to collaborate. When we're going through a tough time, we can circle the drain, spiraling around the question, *What is even the point of all this?* Awe points us to the answer. It says, *This. Just this, right here.*

TIMING
Anytime.

SUPPLIES

- A nice place outside
- A blanket to sit or lie down on
- A timer
- A journal

1. Find a place outside where you can sit or lie down on the ground, undisturbed, for several minutes. Close your eyes and orient to the sounds for a moment. Imagine any irritating sounds just fading into the background of your awareness. Scan for the sounds you enjoy more— the breeze, the birds—and focus on those for a few cycles of breath.

2. Remember a time you enjoyed a wonderful experience of Awe, or even just witnessed someone else experiencing Awe. The secondhand experience doesn't even have to be real for your body to have a response—we can let our mirror neurons do the work. I like to think about the scene in *Barbie* when Margot Robbie's character is on the bench in the park, getting her first real look at real people living real lives in the Real World. She's overcome by beauty and touched by humanness. (Not me crying again . . . *grabs tissue* . . .)

3. After a few moments of enlivening your awareness with memories of Awe, open your eyes and look down

at the ground. Focus on a small, specific area, like a single square foot of Earth. Set a timer and for the next 15 minutes, don't take your eyes off this tiny section of the Earth. Give it your full attention the entire time, and wait. Wait for it . . . keep breathing and looking. At some point, you might discover something awesome right in that little space. It might be the work of a beautiful beetle you hadn't noticed before. It could be the sheer number of grains of sand. It could be anything, but as soon as you start to notice wonder or delight or enchantment, you're getting close. Don't rush through or skip to the next step. Hang out in the good stuff until your timer goes off.

4. Once the timer goes off, set it again for another 15 minutes. Now look up at the sky. Take in every square inch of the sky. Let your mind wander in outer space. Look down at yourself, little miraculous you, making your way through the vastness of the Cosmos. What are the chances? If you start to feel overwhelmed, or too small and vulnerable, come back down to your little patch of Earth and ground yourself there. But if you start to feel enveloped in love, expanded with Awe, give into it. Soften your muscles. Release your need to control it. Let loose a long exhale. Let yourself be enfolded into the miracle of Life.

You're terrific.

Your mere existence is delightful and amazing.

How did you even get here, you?

Welcome to Earth. This is your home. You belong. We're glad you're here.

5. To close this ritual, you may want to journal your experience, thoughts, and feelings. Trust your pages to be a big enough container to hold all that.

Author's Notes

1 Shiota, Lani. "How Awe Transforms the Body and Mind." The Greater Good Science Center. Accessed January 30, 2024. Video, 59:06. https://www.youtube.com/watch?v=uW8h3JIMmVQ.

Balance

Be Seaweed

Though we often turn to the Earth element for grounding in turbulent times, Earth can be slow to find its level. Sometimes Water is a more effective ally in finding Balance. Some upheavals require the spaciousness of an oceanic ritual container. Sometimes we'd prefer a little less gravity. This remedy helps us find an equilibrium between tethered and floaty, secure and drifting, grounded and fluid.[1]

TIMING

Enhance this remedy by practicing daily for a week to the rhythm of the lunar day, which is 24 hours and 50 minutes long. If you start on a Sunday at 10:00 AM, shifting forward by 50 minutes each day, that means by Saturday your start time would be 3:00 PM.[2] It also pairs nicely with the Full Moon.

SUPPLIES

- A small white bowl of water with enough salt added that it tastes like the sea

1. Stand with your feet about hip-width apart, shoulders rolled back so your spine is strong, with your chin parallel to the earth. Breathe naturally as you sense the energy trickling down in your body into your feet and ankles, filling your legs. You don't have to work to direct it, simply be patient and allow gravity to do the work. When you feel quite aware of your feet feeling solidly on the ground, picture yourself standing at the edge of the ocean on a Full Moon night.

2. Dip your fingers into the salt water and draw a line on your skin from hip to hip. This is your horizon line. Everything below is the ocean, everything above is the starry sky. Say aloud,

    The Picatrix instructs us.[3] "The Moon should be asked for fluidity of movements, disclosure of secrets, abundance of waters, extinguishing of fires . . . "

    I ask you, Moon, to grant me Balance.

    Let your entire body soften as you imagine yourself made up of ocean and sky. With your feet firmly planted, let your body sway to the currents of the ocean, sensing yourself held in perfect suspension between the ocean floor and the Moon.

3. Imagine yourself now as a single stem of bull kelp, the lower end holding fast to the ocean floor, the top end floating and free flowing. Notice how it feels to be fluid yet balanced.

Dip the fingers of both hands in the salt water and draw parallel lines from your middle toe of each foot, up your legs to the horizon line of your body at your hips. From there, merge the lines together and draw a single saltwater line up your torso, throat, under your chin, to the tip of your nose, between your eyes, all the way up to the crown of your head, like in this image.

Stand for a moment sensing this alignment even as your body sways with the never-ending currents of the ocean. Feel yourself bobbing along like bull kelp, securely attached below, fluid and free above, aligned, held steady yet in motion.[4]

Be seaweed. . . . Just pretend. . . . Allow your upper body to sway in the healing waters and decide whether you'd like your feet to remain planted on the ocean floor or if you'd like to move about the room, floating along as seaweed in the currents. Explore how you can be both balanced and in motion at the same time. Float in the Womb of the World for a while.

4. When you feel complete, come back to stillness in a standing position. Dip your fingers into the saltwater

and draw waves on your arms, your torso, your legs, anywhere you can reach.

You are Water. You are ruled by the Moon. The Moon knows the rhythm of Balance.

Thank the Moon for holding space for you. Notice how it feels to balance Earth and Water energies to find groundedness.

Author's Notes

1   This ritual is inspired by the work of Philip Shepherd which he calls The Embodied Presence Process (TEPP) and shares in workshops and his writings. Shepherd, Philip. *Radical Wholeness: The Embodied Present and the Ordinary Grace of Being.* North Atlantic Books, 2017.

2   Here's the science of the lunar day according to the National Ocean Service: "Unlike a 24-hour solar day, a lunar day lasts 24 hours and 50 minutes. This occurs because the moon revolves around the Earth in the same direction that the Earth is rotating on its axis. Therefore, it takes the Earth an extra 50 minutes to 'catch up' to the moon. Since the Earth rotates through two tidal 'bulges' every lunar day, we experience two high and two low tides every 24 hours and 50 minutes." "Tides and Water Levels." NOAA's National Ocean Service. Accessed November 2, 2023. https://oceanservice. noaa.gov/education/tutorial_tides/media/supp_tide05.html.

3   The *Picatrix* is a 400-page book on astrological magic written in Arabic sometime around the middle of the 11th century. "Picatrix." Wikipedia. Accessed November 2, 2023. https://en.wikipedia.org/ wiki/Picatrix. It has recently experienced a bit of a modern renaissance. Learn more in the first episode of my AstroMagic Miniseries

on *The Numinous Podcast* with astrologer, Eliza Robertson: Podcast episode "AstroMagic Miniseries with Eliza Robertson and the Sun." *The Numinous Podcast.* https://crspagnola.podbean.com/e/tnp198 -astro-magic-miniseries-with-eliza-robertson-and-the-sun/.

al-Majrītī, Maslamah ibn Aḥmad. *Picatrix: A Medieval Treatise on Astral Magic.* Pennsylvania State University Press, 2019.

4   As always, if any part of this practice is physically unavailable to you, such as standing, supporting your weight for a period of time, or closing your eyes while swaying, you can absolutely achieve significant effects by doing it seated or in your mind.

Celebration

Little Lifts

Before he died in 2019, my Quaker elder, Michael, and I would meet regularly for tea and spiritual friendship. I once asked Michael how he would answer the question from the famous Proust questionnaire, *What do you consider perfect happiness?*

"The little lift," he said. "It happens all the time. The little lift. That's what happiness is. Happiness is not some big thing that we can gather in and hold to our breast, no. It's the little lift and it's available most of the time, everywhere . . . Walking in the sunshine, walking in the rain, being with somebody I care about . . . lots of little lifts."

In turbulent times when good news and elevated mood are hard to come by, celebrating the Little Lifts becomes all the more important. Celebration releases a host of chemicals that are profoundly valuable to our well-being and long-term health: Endorphins give us that giddy feeling of being on top of the world, serotonin is the rocket booster for joy, and dopamine gives us the satisfaction of accomplishment.

Celebration serves a biological impulse to witness and be witnessed, to spread our joy around, and to strengthen our bond by putting our love on display for everyone to see. As Michael put it, "We create a substance among ourselves—we call it our marriage, our friendship, we call it our [Quaker] Meeting . . . This substance is not us, and it's not visible, but it is tangible. It's tangible to a loving heart."[1] Celebration is a way to give form to the substance we create among ourselves. It provides a vessel for what's in our hearts to extend outward into our relationships.

I love celebrating in big ways: food, flowers, formal place settings, the whole nine yards. Spectacle! Audience! Grand gestures! (Tell me you're a Leo Moon without telling me you're a Leo Moon.) Whereas my husband (Aries Moon) is more of a *Watch me dive!* kind of person. He wants an on-demand supply of inexhaustible enthusiasm while I gaze upon his mighty works for a few minutes. He wants me to *ooh* and *ahh*, and offer positive appraisal. No muss, no fuss, just a moment of adoration. Somewhere in the middle, we compromised on the *Huzzah!* as part of our daily rhythm.

Whenever we notice a Little Lift, we'll inject some Celebration into the moment and loudly cheer, *Huzzah!* as we throw our hands in the air. You submitted the report? *Huzzah!* You got the folded laundry into the drawers? *Huzzah!!* The fancy ice cream is on sale? *Huzzah!!!*

We do it for almost anything, no matter how small.[2] It's a way to savor the goodness of the day. It injects levity into life. It's a great mood booster. Importantly, it exercises our brain, challenging us to orient to feelings of love, appreciation, pleasure, and satisfaction. There's magic in this moment—you're casting a spell to attract more joy into your life. Plus, free dopamine in this economy? Sign me up!

TIMING
Every day.

SUPPLIES
- Just your observant and willing self is needed, but enlisting others is fun

1. Choose a celebratory word such as *Huzzah!*, *Ta-da!*, *Woot woot!*, *Boo-ya!*, *Hey-oh!*, *Woo-hoo!*, *Yippee!*, or *Hooray!*.

2. For one day, say it all the time for every little thing.

3. For the next five days, say it thoughtfully whenever you experience a Little Lift—slow down and really savor it.

4. On the seventh day, celebrate yourself in a bigger way.[3] Bake yourself a cake, connect with friends, raise a toast, and have a round of applause to recognize

yourself for having spent a full week building your resilience through Celebration.[4] Huzzah to you!

IT MIGHT BE HARDER THAN YOU EXPECT

How does your body react to Celebration? Is it easy or uncomfortable to inhabit this energy? Do you roll your eyes and shrug it off quickly? Is it getting more fun or sincere with practice? Do you find yourself craving more enthusiasm and celebratory energy from others? Take note. This is good data for you (and maybe for your therapist).

Author's Notes

1   Listen to this conversation: Michael Phillips, interview by Carmen Spagnola: "Community, Autonomy + Forgiveness." *The Numinous Podcast*, episode 33. Accessed February 8, 2024. https://crspagnola.podbean.com/e/tnp33-community-autonomy-forgiveness-with-michael-phillips/.

   Michael Phillips, interview by Carmen Spagnola: "Grieving for Susan + Civilization." *The Numinous Podcast*, episode 24. Accessed February 8, 2024. https://crspagnola.podbean.com/e/tnp24-grieving-for-susan-civilization-with-michael-phillips/.

2   People who are parsimonious with their praise should practice this remedy every day, as often as possible, with extra emphasis

on major milestones and life events. Perfectionists will also benefit enormously from this. Choose a celebratory exclamation and run with it. Most important is to make this an everyday thing: Scan your day for Little Lifts and celebrate them.

3 Celebrations that consist of three main things, recognition, food and drink, and other people, contribute to prosocial feelings and a sense of community support. Brick, D. J., Wight, K. G., Bettman, J. R., Chartrand, T. L., and Fitzsimons, G. J. "Celebrate Good Times: How Celebrations Increase Perceived Social Support." *Journal of Public Policy & Marketing* 42, no. 2 (2023): 115–32. DOI: 10.1177/07439156221145696.

4 Humans the world over have sought collective joy through ecstatic dance and feasting since ancient times, and the elites have tried to quash it every time—from the early days of Christianity as a "danced religion" to the persecution of the Sufis to the criminalization of Indigenous peoples' potlatches by European colonizers in North America. No sooner do the people start dancing than the powerful start punishing. In turbulent times, you may take to the street for a political action, only to find yourself singing and dancing as a form of reclamation and resistance. Defiant celebration to protest oppression has been seen in Iran as part of the Woman, Life, Freedom movement, in the Black Lives Matter actions in the United States, and in the One Billion Rising campaign in Southeast Asia. Celebration is a mechanism through which we survive adversity together, and it helps heal collective wounds as much as personal ones. Ehrenreich, Barbara. *Dancing in the Streets: A History of Collective Joy.* Henry Holt and Company, 2007.

Connection

Love Spell for One

This remedy is a love spell to enlarge inner reservoirs of warmth and tenderness, and build up tolerance for staying in Connection. A lot of us believe we need more Connection but then get flustered, freeze, and shrink away from it when it happens. Here is a simple process you can do in under a minute a day to build your Connection muscles.[1]

The ally you call on should be an animal or human with really lovely, kind eyes, a Competent Protector who is strong and safeguards you from harm.[2] They're the type that will throw themselves between you and danger. They'll never let anyone hurt you. They're also nurturing and gentle with you. They offer comfort and succor when you're downtrodden or alone. You love them in an uncomplicated way. They can be real or made up, alive or dead, a cultural icon or a character from fiction. When they look at you, their eyes seem to beam the message, You are so wonderful and so precious to me.

Some people struggle to decide on a Competent Protector who fits this criteria. They flounder with a Goldilocks indecision, inviting in allies then deciding they're not quite right. The solution is to find a good enough ally, not a perfect one. You should do this practice daily and experiment with different allies so that you've got a whole crew you can call on if you need them.

Some folks have attachment wounds that won't allow them to relax or make eye contact with an ally in human form. I'm so sorry if that's the case for you. You deserve so much better than that. You of all people will benefit from this remedy. If you can muster the courage to try, I suggest you start by calling in animal protectors, especially mammals known for communal care, such as Horse, Dog, Deer, Wolf, Bear, Lion, Buffalo, Elephant, Monkey, Beaver, Squirrel, Rabbit, and Sheep.[3]

You can enhance the magic of this remedy by doing it on Friday, the day ruled by Venus, patron of love and connection.

SUPPLIES
- Bathroom mirror
- Bar of soap
- A face cloth wetted with warm water

1. Stand in front of the mirror and use the bar of soap to draw a circle around your image that encompasses your entire head.

2. Close your eyes. Tune in to your body to get a baseline of your present state. Then call in your Competent Protector and notice how that feels.

3. Allow your Competent Protector to look upon you with kind eyes and shower their love on you. Keep breathing as you receive their kindness and Connection. What's it like to permit yourself to be seen through loving eyes?

4. Still with your eyes closed, imagine you look them in the eye. Even if it's quick like a blink in reverse, just take a peek. Look at them looking at you with kind eyes. Be with the loving gaze for a moment.

5. Allow this loving gaze to envelope you. Let it soften your muscles and restore your cells. Let it permeate you like a golden light that reaches to your core. Bathe in the glow.

6. With the warm face cloth, gently wash your face. Cleanse the residue of all other gazes that were not loving. All harshness, criticism, rejection, cruelty,

anything that made you feel inferior or disconnected from your true self; all that is now cleansed and you are purified.

7. Open your eyes and look at your reflection in the mirror. Gaze upon yourself with kind eyes. Use the wet cloth to wash the soapy circle away, dissolving the distorted ways you've seen and judged yourself. Once the mirror is clean, use your finger to draw a heart around your image. Look at yourself for a moment more with kind eyes. This helps increase your tolerance for receiving love.

8. Thank your Competent Protector and say goodbye to them for now. Be reassured knowing they watch over you with a loving gaze every moment of your life, just because you're you.

Author's Notes

1 Actually the "muscle" we're building is the tone in the social engagement branch of the nervous system, known as the ventral vagus. The linkages run from the brain to our face, especially around the eyes, mouth, jaw, and ears. We can increase our vagal tone, and therefore our capacity for social engagement, in many ways, but the most direct (and for some of us, most challenging) is through sharing contact nutrition—eye contact, soothing tone of voice and

resonant language, safe touch, shared rhythm, and ingestion behaviors like eating and drinking—with others. I first heard the term "contact nutrition" in a training with Diane Poole Heller in 2017.

2 This remedy is in part inspired by the work of Diane Poole Heller who developed Dynamic Attachment Re-Patterning. Trauma Solutions: Diane Poole Heller. Accessed February 1, 2024. https://dianepooleheller.com.

3 Some neurodivergent folks who struggle with eye contact benefit from this remedy because of its gentle, indirect approach. Others who recoil at being perceived, yet wish to increase their tolerance for connection, should keep it short and sweet. Two minutes max.

Conservation

Gift to the Future

This remedy is an anchor to embeddedness, heritage, and emplacement. In turbulent times, it's comforting to tap into the courage, resilience, and creativity of our Ancestors. In the process, we revive and embody the wisdom of how our people lived in reciprocity with the Land and the More Than Human in specific places over time.

"Cultural conservation" is a term that describes the measures we take to preserve and safeguard the traditional knowledge, skills, language, songs, oral history, customs, foods, festivals, and lifeways that we most value and cherish. These touchstones enhance the quality of our humanness and contribute as much to beauty, pleasure, self-understanding, and belonging as they do to practical survival and endurance.

This remedy takes some time. You might say it takes generations. You'll need to research a lineage, practice, or a place you're drawn to. (Let's collect these under a "cultural artifact" umbrella.) You'll need to find experts with living connections to this cultural artifact and initiate a genuine relationship with them.[1] You'll want to spend time with them and learn all you can. You'll repay them somehow and ensure fair exchange for their lifetime of experience. You should keep doing this until you become competent enough with this cultural artifact that you can transmit it to others.

What of your family history, or of this present moment in the world do you hope will continue into the future? Your Nonna's cookie recipe? The knots you learned at summer camp? Sand casting for jewelry? The myths that match the seasons of the Wheel of the Year in your culture? This remedy has led me to learn Scottish Gaelic laments that I've sung at the bedside of the dying. I've learned ancestral skills like canning, fire starting, and hide tanning. I'm now familiar with the Indigenous languages of most places I've ever lived including Hul'q'umi'num, lək̓ʷəŋiʔnəŋ, and Nsyilxcən.

Maybe you hope the world always has embroidery, wheat weaving, pottery, celestial navigation, home birthing practices, morse code, haiku, illuminated manuscripts, erhu players, cheese caves, homemade jam, ceremonial dances and songs, moonshine, herbal medicine, or handmade log houses. You need to learn, then. Not everything, but pick a special something. Whatever cultural artifact you wish to be carried forward into the future, begin to carry it now. It will bring you joy and soothing, and will help pass the time as you wait for the turbulent times to sort themselves out.

Begin as soon as you can.

SUPPLIES
- A curious mind and willingness to not necessarily become great at it, but commit to stewarding knowledge of it, nonetheless

1. Ask yourself, *What do I wish to conserve for future generations?*

2. Take the next natural step toward learning, improving, or sharing.[2] Do not allow perfectionism to slow your progress. Work alongside other learners and share knowledge. Absorb all you can from elders about the topic.

3. Share what you know. Share it in the folk way, not as an expert—share it from the heart, with generosity and pride. Allow this remedy to enhance your pleasure, affirm your joy, and be a message to the future about who you are, what you love, and the values you hold dear.

Author's Notes

1 YouTube can be an amazing resource for folks who don't have access to elders or wisdom keepers in their lineage.

2 The Natural Step Framework includes the process of "backcasting" where you work backward from an imagined vision of future success. If you're not sure which cultural artifact you want to focus on, you might spend some time envisioning the future you wish for. From there, work your way back in time, noting all the key steps that would need to occur for that future to unfold, until you arrive back here in the now. What is the first natural step you would need to take from here? "Backcasting." The Natural Step (Canada). Accessed January 7, 2024. https://www.naturalstep.ca/backcasting.

3 This is a great remedy for healing from perfectionism—learn to revel in being kind of shit at something but doing it anyway, just for the love of it. By extension, this becomes a remedy for unconscious or internalized white supremacy since perfectionism is a key feature of white supremacy culture. This is especially true if you're white and you choose a cultural artifact rooted in a specific place where your wayback people came from before they were acculturated into whiteness. See www.whitesupremacyculture.info to explore Tema Okun's work on white supremacy culture. See also whiteawake.org for ancestral recovery courses like "Before We Were White" and "Roots Deeper Than Whiteness."

Movement

Soft Animals

For all the wonders of technology and modernity, it's good sometimes to remember that we're all just little mammals making our way in a big world. Like cats and rats and elephants, humans essentially need only food, water, shelter, and each other to survive. Free of oppression and left to our own ingenuity, mere survival is not so hard. It's the emotional weight of living that becomes grueling at times.

To fill our hearts with the will to carry on, it helps to prime the pump by moving our arms and legs. Even just a bit. This remedy for a listless heart involves intuitive Movement to reconnect with our instinctual nature. It can be done in bed or on the couch, even better if you can make a soft mat of blankets on the floor. You can even do it as you awake in the morning to give getting out of bed a bit more flair.

Music is really helpful for this process, especially cinematic scores, ones that have a strong storytelling quality to them rather than a repetitive beat—more like a musical narrative arc than a dance track.[1] Music is like having an improv partner—you can *Yes, And!* your way from freeze into social engagement with life.[2]

The only rule is to always keep one part of your body in motion for the duration of a song—even if it's just a hand or one finger. Stay in motion, responding to the music and whatever impulse arises. Even if what arises is a *Fuck no I'm not doing that*. That's great—follow that instinct and do the Movement that feels like recoil or a firm *No*. Build on the Yeses and Nos and keep your body in motion. Trust your body. Permit its desires. No censoring yourself, no performing, no fancy moves. Whenever you need to rest, rest. Just three or four minutes is plenty of practice.

TIMING
I like to do this practice earlier in the day so I'm not fighting the inertia of a midafternoon slump.

SUPPLIES
- Somewhere you can lie down or move comfortably on all fours

1. Start the music and lie on your back with your eyes closed. Say to your heart, *Thank you for safe passage through the night*.[3] Twinkle your fingers and toes for a while.

2. Gradually incorporate more of your legs and arms. You can even roll over onto your side, tummy, or onto your hands and knees. Try to keep your body more or less horizontal and low to the ground, more animal-like, less bipedal.

   What kind of mammal do you feel like today? How does the soft animal of your body want to move right now?[4] Maybe you feel restless like a tiger or slow like an elephant. Maybe you feel aquatic like a manatee, dolphin, or whale . . . let the Movement be intuitive and sincere, without agenda or goal. Don't worry about how it looks.

3. When you feel complete, slowly stand up. Standing up is a primal signal to your body that you are alive, that you are not prey, that you are capable, and you have the power to act on your desires.[5] Say to your heart, *Thank you in advance for safe passage through the day.*

Author's Notes

1   I use the soundtrack to *Prehistoric Planet*. Anže Rozman, Kara Talve, Hans Zimmer. *Prehistoric Planet: Season 1*. Lakeshore Records, 2022, MP3.
2   *Yes, And!* is a classic theatre sports exercise to develop improv skills. The rule of the game is that no matter what your performance partner throws at you, you must accept their idea and build on it. If they

say, *It's raining cats and dogs!* you can't say, *No it's not, it's a hundred degrees out here!* You have to say something like, *Yes! And I wonder why all the animals are running for higher ground—should we get in a boat?* And then the other person should say, *YES WE SHOULD, because that's the first sign of a tsunami!* Ha ha; it's a fun game.

3   Thanks to my friend, Monique Gray Smith for this language. I address my morning thanks both to the Great Mother Spirit Creator that I believe in, and to my heart which kept me alive while I slept. Obviously, you can phrase this thanks to your gods and/or your heart in whatever way works for you.

4   This is a reference to the poem, "Wild Geese," by Mary Oliver, patron saint of this Soft Animals practice. Oliver, Mary. *Wild Geese: Selected Poems.* Bloodaxe, 2004.

5   If standing isn't available to you, look up or reach up as your signal of aliveness, capability, and power.

Nurturance

Cocooning

Surrendering to change is a core collapse skill, yet the urge to tense up, grip, and brace can be intense. As we grow up and encounter a sometimes threatening world, our ability to yield is diminished. It becomes difficult to relax into a sense of safety. In Body Mind Centering, the ability to surrender is one of the five components in early movement development (often referred to as the Satisfaction Cycle): to yield, reach, grasp, pull, and push.[1]

As infants, we enter the world yielding as we rest in the amniotic sac, held by gravity and the waters of the womb. Eventually we begin to explore our body and the world through the other movements which build upon each other, enabling us to crawl, walk, and run. But yielding comes first. To yield facilitates rest, the state we return to after all that movement and effort, and which restores us before the next round of activity.

With this remedy we create a nurturing cocoon in order to recover our ability to yield and rest.[2] Though you can definitely achieve some effectiveness on your own, it's best if you can enlist a trusted friend to help. Everybody deserves to experience the sweetness of a nurturing cocoon and it can be fun to take turns building them together. This spell works on people of all ages and abilities, genders and bodies, and histories.[3] The magic of this remedy is surprisingly profound.

TIMING

Please, at least once more in your life, allow yourself to yield into Nurturance. Consider repeating this ritual a few times to see just how soft you can become.

SUPPLIES

- Several pillows of different sizes
- A hot water bottle or heating pad (optional)
- Eye pillow (optional)
- Several soft blankets of varying weights
- A large space where you can comfortably recline such as the sofa or the floor[4]
- A playlist of gentle music lasting at least 15 minutes

1. Set your intention to be open to Nurturance from the Greater Benevolent Powers. These can include Ancestors, deities, and allies from the spirit realm. Press your hand against your left lung and affirm, *I yield control and am open to receive.*[5]

2. Place a line of pillows down and lie on your side with your back against them. The pillows should be touching you from the back of your head to your tailbone. Tuck your legs up in a comfortable fetal position and place a pillow between your knees. Place the hot water bottle either near your belly or your feet. Hug another pillow against your chest. It's important that the entire back of your body and the entire front of your body have contact with a pillow or some light pressure. If you have an eye pillow, that can be nice, too.

3. Imagine there are angelic beings draping you with soft blankets now. Cover yourself with the blankets so that only your face is left visible, ensuring good airflow. Ask to be tucked in or layer on more blankets until you feel as comfortable as possible.

   Spend some time settling, feeling yourself completely enveloped in care. Be curious about your internal experience. How does it feel in this cocoon? Does it feel safe enough to soften your muscles a little bit more? Would you like to reach out and hold your helper's hand?

4. Turn on the gentle music. While it plays, go into heavy mode by relaxing your muscles everywhere you can. With each exhale, melt into a global micro-relaxation

as you continue to soften your muscles. Sense the Nurturance flowing to you from the Greater Powers, more and more as you continue to soften.

5. When the playlist is finished, you might be asleep or you may feel refreshed. Many people feel as though they don't want to come out. Remember, you can do this again, at any time, and as often as you need. Press your hand to your left lung and thank the Greater Benevolent Powers and your helper if you had one.

Author's Notes

1   Body Mind Centering is a form of somatic psychology developed by Bonnie Bainbridge Cohen. "Bonnie Bainbridge Cohen." Body-Mind Centering. Accessed January 5, 2024. https://www.body mindcentering.com/about/bonnie-bainbridge-cohen/.

2   This technique from NeuroAffective Touch Therapy is called Creating a Nurture Surround. NeuroAffective Touch Institute. Accessed February 1, 2024. https://neuroaffectivetouch.com.

     NeuroAffective Touch was developed by Aline LaPierre who also coauthored a book on the NeuroAffective Relational Model (NARM) of developmental trauma recovery.

     Heller, Laurence, LaPierre, Aline. *Healing Developmental Trauma: How Early Trauma Affects Self-Regulation, Self-Image, and the Capacity for Relationship.* North Atlantic Books, 2012.

3   This remedy can be especially good for folks experiencing sleep disturbances such as difficulty falling asleep, nightmares, wakefulness, and insomnia. Parents whose kids struggle to sleep can allow the

child to make a cocoon for the adult(s) first, which associates sleep with fun and maybe even a little envy. Ask if the child would like to be cocooned and see how it goes—it may need to happen in stages over several days or weeks.

Remember, you're not having a therapy session. If you sense yourself getting pulled deeply into the experience, pull back a bit. Stay in the shallows. You want to be able to hold space for your friend when it's their turn. Suggest some transition time and pull out your journal if themes come up that you want to debrief later with a counselor.

4   Be thoughtful about the location. Sometimes beds or bedrooms are a site of harm, stress, or trauma, so some people may find it impossible to relax there. It might be better to place an air mattress on the living room floor with tons of blankets on top for cushioning or do this on the sofa.

5   We place our hand over the left lung because there is a branch of the vagus nerve that runs through this area, the place where we often symbolically locate our heart. Applying a safe light touch here can have a calming, soothing effect on the body.

Pronking

Stayin' Alive

Pronking is a real word and a real thing that mammals do when they are in a state of empowerment or triumph. Hold an image in your mind of a baby goat bouncing around a yard and you'll have a sense of what I mean. Humans do it when we're really feeling ourselves. Pronking is giving *RuPaul's Drag Race*.[1] It's giving *John Travolta–Stayin' Alive–Saturday Night Fever*. It's giving *I'm The Shit*.

It's also a healthy stage in stress management. To successfully escape from a threat, our body needs to discharge the pent-up tension. We use that discharge to get the heck outta there, and then we look around like, *Did you just see that? Holy crap! That was wild! I barely got out in time! Nice work, Me!* then strut away with a bounce in our step. We also do it when some sort of daring-do works out well for us, like when a skateboarder finally lands a trick. This is Pronking.

Our triumphant escape enables a felt sense of safety that then facilitates an exploratory orientation to the world. After we Pronk, we can attend to the world with curiosity, creativity, and collaboration. Perhaps more importantly, the more we Pronk, the more we refill our reserves of vitality, inspiration, and sense of vibrancy.

After the discharge of autonomic arousal, our body will naturally start to bounce a little. Pronking has an up-and-down and side-to-side motion to it that's really fun! We swish our hair, sway our hips, and walk with a bounce in our step. Our face is animated and our eyes beam with confident, even flirty, vibes. We want to get it on with life! There's an inward rush of vitality (empowerment!) that we distribute through the body with a shimmy.[2]

Unfortunately, capitalism has trained us to channel this Pronking state into productivity and consumer activities. We get a surge of energy and inspiration that often leads to shopping. We have an urge to leverage this vim and vigor that, sadly, is all too quickly squandered on emails, cleaning, or tackling projects. Quite understandably, if you're someone who has chronic low energy or disability, your first impulse might be to harness this vitality to accomplish overdue tasks.

Can I ask you to just hold on a minute, though? We can do much more with this moment than just work or do chores or spend money on shiny things.

I encourage you to just Pronk for a bit first. Don't move too quickly toward tasking. Let yourself have a moment to enjoy the feeling of life force energy rushing back into your body.[3] Let it permeate your cells. Let this joyful triumphant feeling imprint itself on your muscles, fascia, and skin. Let it become part of your DNA.

If you can hang out in the Pronking state for even just two minutes, you give your brain a chance to have a neuroplastic event. In other words, your brain gets some time to create new neural pathways. This allows your brain to revisit this feeling more easily in the future. Pronking is a way to reinforce our capacity for survival and success, and so we should cultivate this feeling whenever it's available. It's a felt sense of our own competence—a critical boost of confidence in our ability to navigate turbulent times.

Now, Pronking isn't a remedy you can artificially simulate or force. That's why there's no step-by-step instruction for this remedy. You have to have that feeling of successful escape to spur it on. The good thing (if you can call it good) is that it's not all that uncommon for our body to respond to a relatively mundane task as though it is a life threat. There are lots of opportunities for Pronking if we recognize the tension we carry over everyday stressors like saying no to a request, setting a boundary, receiving feedback, or speaking up in a group. Every time you do a hard thing, you should Pronk about it after.

Those of us who were raised with a lot of criticism or were admonished to be humble may repress the natural urge toward Pronking. We might habitually downplay or skip over our emotions and avoid exuberance. In that case, the physical signs of Pronking can be extremely subtle.

Watch for a slight scrunch of the nose in an *aw-shucks* kind of way. A tiny shrug of the shoulders. A puckering of the mouth that wants to smile but isn't allowed. Notice yourself feeling feisty. Amplify Pronking behaviors like cocking your head, tossing your hair, speaking with a playful cadence, jutting your hips, bouncing a little, and then give yourself permission to just do it. Pronk away! Put on some music to help you. Unleash your inner vogue dancer and have fun!

Author's Notes

1   "It's giving" is a catchphrase that originates in 1990s New York queer, Black, and Latina ballroom culture and African American Vernacular English, and has now entered common parlance. It's a slang term used to describe the particular vibe that something is emitting.

2   Cellularjuesus. "Springbok pronking." YouTube video. Uploaded April 20, 2013. Accessed February 8, 2024. https://youtu.be/jMIi B9DnRXg?si=oWkNbvss2KWsDHbH.

3   Remember that scene in *Jerry Maguire* after Jerry dramatically quits his job and he's driving in his car? He's punching buttons on the radio looking for a station with a good song, but he can't find one that fits the moment. *He wants to Pronk,* but he can't figure out how. His Pronk is nearly thwarted until he finally finds Tom Petty's "Free Fallin'" and belts it out. Sweet relief!

Protection

Shielding Bag

Everyone deserves to feel protected, everywhere, at all times, but especially within the walls of our own home. This remedy involves giving honor, focus, and priority to your basic needs so that you can flourish. It will help to anchor a sense of Protection in and around your personal space.[1]

Regular ongoing Protection practices should be part of our spiritual hygiene regimen. This can include prayer or protective amulets that we create for specific situations. Consider durable, long-lasting spellcraft for this.[2] Hang mirrors in strategic areas indoors and out to deflect negative influences from the street. Anoint your keyholes with garlic-infused olive oil to prevent restless spirits from entering. Install a lucky statuary or guardian deity at your front door. Plant medicinal flowers, shrubs, and herbs to create a spiritually potent boundary along the street or up your front walk.

If you feel like you need to upgrade your home's spiritual security system, make four spell jars—one for each corner of the house.[3] Place a sprig of protective herb and a few sharp steel pins into each jar, speak the name of a fierce guardian deity into each, seal them with wax, and bury them at the four corners of your property, or at the cardinal directions outside your house, or place them in the corners of your room.

While this type of spellcraft is effective and definitely needed at times, it occurs outside of ourselves and relies on faith, so it doesn't always make us *feel* protected. A feel-

PROTECTIVE PLANTS

Bay: Cleanses; has triumphant qualities

Fennel: Dispels malefic spirits

Juniper: Banishes heaviness, blesses householders

Mugwort: Invokes Artemis, protector of girls and women

Rosehip: Invites friendly spirits to take up residence

Rosemary: Purifies, protects, uplifts

Thyme: Soothes nerves, prevents misfortune, brings good luck

Pepper: Removes spiritual contamination quickly

ing of Protection arises when we are safe, seen, secure, and soothed. This may seem aspirational to some, especially those living in a dangerous environment. Still, it's a worthy aim. Orienting toward feelings of safeness is a skill that we might need to learn and make an extra effort to cultivate so that we can lean into liberation when the opportunity arises. When we feel protected, we're more likely to take risks to grow and develop, come into our true self-expression, and thrive. In order to feel protected, we need to break it down into specific parts we can build on.

To feel safe, we need to know that no physical, emotional, psychological, or spiritual harm will come to us. What could be a symbol of safety for you? Maybe a lock and key, or some jewelry from a beloved Ancestor.

To feel seen, we need to know that our whole self is welcome and appreciated, not just the parts that people like the most or are comfortable with—our whole self must be included for us to feel truly seen. Are there parts of you that you wish were seen and appreciated? Find a symbol to represent parts of yourself you wish to be welcomed, cherished, and protected.

To feel secure, we need to know that people will act with congruence and consistency. They are who they appear to be, and do what they say they'll do. They might make mistakes, but they won't keep things from us or gaslight us.

Gather something to symbolize truth and integrity such as a rock or a clear quartz crystal.

To feel soothed, we need to know that our preferences matter, that others will attune to us, and obligingly meet our needs. We need to be comforted when we're hurt, not given advice or told to look on the bright side. A heart symbol could be perfect here.

TIMING

Do this on a Monday to petition the Moon and her mistress, Artemis, for Protection. To assert strong boundaries, perform this on a Saturday. Saturn presides over limits and borders.

SUPPLIES

- A drawstring bag big enough to hold your symbolic items

1. Sit with your symbols gathered in front of you, perhaps at your altar. Cradle the bag in the palm of your left hand so both your palm and the bag are open to receive. Close your eyes and take a few settling breaths.

   Call in some loving yet fiercely protective energies. As you sense them drawing near, petition them for guardianship over your personal space and well-being.

Ask them to give extra attention to your safekeeping, to shelter you in their care, and take you in under the auspice of their magical sphere of influence.

2. Using your right hand, place your symbol for safety in the bag. Affirm,

   I am open to receiving Protection and Safety.

   Note the change in the palm of your left hand, even if subtle.

   Place your symbol for feeling seen in your left hand. Affirm,

   I am open to the welcome of my true and whole self.

   Place your symbol of security in the bag. Affirm,

   I am open to dependable support.

   Place your symbol of soothing in the bag. Affirm,

   I am receptive to comfort and soothing.

3. Feel the weight of the bag in your left palm for a moment, then clutch the bag to your chest, holding it with both hands. Affirm,

   I deserve to be protected, safe, seen, secure, and soothed.

4. Slowly draw the bag closed, saying aloud,

   I restrict access to any and all who threaten my safety, invalidate my existence, violate my trust, or minimize my needs.

Place your drawstring bag either on your altar, beside your bed, on your desk, near your front door, or anywhere else you'd like to amplify protective powers. Close by affirming,

I am a child of earth and starry sky. I am protected by the Greater Benevolent Powers whose inviolable law is Love. My prayer is their joy and my vision shall come. And so it is.[4]

Author's Notes

1 In my career, I've helped several women escape abusive relationships. Very often, the first place we begin is orienting to safeness and asserting agency on the spiritual level. We set energetic boundaries first and call in protective forces. This remedy can be a very private, internal process. You can do it. I believe you, and I believe in you. You deserve to feel safe, seen, secure, and soothed. It may not feel within reach right now, but this is your birthright. Brigid's mantle be upon you, Artemis protect you, Hekate avenge you, Inanna raise you up.

2 This is common in feng shui, a traditional Chinese method of creating harmonious spaces. In Norse tradition, the resident house elf may have a statue outside the home. We see something similar with house poles in several Coast Salish cultures. In terms of plantings, I like to have Rosemary at the front of my home and Nettle in the backyard. That way, whoever/whatever enters is cleansed and purified, and there's always protection at my back.

3 See *The Spirited Kitchen* for more on spells jars: Spagnola, Carmen. *The Spirited Kitchen: Recipes and Rituals for the Wheel of the Year.* Countryman Press, 2022.

4 "I am a child of earth and starry sky" is from the Orphic Hymns

according to author and translator, Kristin Mathis. "AstroMagic Miniseries: Kristin Mathis, Venus, and the Orphic Hymns." *The Numinous Podcast*. Podcast episode. Accessed February 6, 2024. https://crspagnola.podbean.com/e/tnp202-astromagic-miniseries-kristin-mathis-venus-and-the-orphic-hymns/.

Renewal

Seeds of Hope

What do you do when you're utterly devoid of resilience, yet life requires you to keep showing up? You ping the Higher Powers to ask for an influx of vigor and stamina. This remedy reminds us that life is irrepressible, with an innate will toward expression. Life will go on and it encourages us to do the same. This remedy is an active prayer for Renewal that taps into a wellspring of Source energy. It involves sacred engagement with the passage of time. It shows us how time partners with life to regenerate hope and heal our heart.

TIMING
Enhance the magic of this remedy by performing it sometime between the New Moon and First Quarter or Waxing Gibbous Moon when the moon is renewing itself. Do it very early in the morning to add another layer of restorative energy, with the gathering vitality of the Sun adding momentum to your magic.

SUPPLIES

- An altar to renewal that may be as simple as a colorful cloth and some space cleared on your dresser
- Paper towel bunched into a ball about the size of your fist when wet
- A small bowl the same diameter as the ball of paper towel
- A sachet of wheat seeds or ¼ cup of wheat berries from an organic grocer
- Water

1. Set your intention for Renewal—to regenerate your vitality, will, energy, commitment, or to reset a waning focus you would like to revive. Prepare your altar to receive your new intention by clearing away any old offerings. Start fresh. Select an altar cloth in a color that reminds you of new life, such as green for sprouting leaves, black for humus soil, red for lifeblood, or gold for divine spark.

2. Prepare your bowl with the ball of wet paper towel. The seeds will grow according to the shape of the towel. I like it to be a curved dome with an overall spherical shape to echo the rising of the sun. Fill a small pitcher or bottle with water.

3. Sit at your altar and meditate on your intention. Envision it coming to pass. How will that feel in your heart, in your belly, in your limbs? What becomes possible when this intention comes to fruition?

4. Pour the seeds on top of the paper towel. Make sure they cover all parts of the dome evenly in one layer. Bless the seeds, saying,

Blessed be the creative, dynamic life force that animates the Cosmos. Blessed be the Source. I call upon Source to [state your intention].

Swell these seeds with renewed energy and fill them with new life.

As the seed grows, so does my vitality.

I bless these seeds with nourishing Waters. I offer my loving attention and care.

Pour the water into the bowl, saying.

Thanks be to the Source of all vitality.

5. Each day, add a splash of water to the bowl so the paper towel remains wet. Speak words of encouragement and love to the seeds as you do. When the wheatgrass grows to about two or three inches high, the spell is complete.[1]

Author's Notes

....

1   To add one more layer of magic to this ritual, cut the wheatgrass and blend it into a fruit smoothie. As you drink, imagine the creative, dynamic life force of the Cosmos entering your body once again, enabling embodied Renewal of your intention.

Wholeness

The Oakness of the Acorn

*My formula for greatness in a human being is amor fati: that one
wants nothing to be different, not forward, not backward, not in
all eternity. Not merely bear what is necessary . . . but love it.*

—Friedrich Nietzsche

The concept of *amor fati,* which can be translated as "love
of one's fate," has been linked to philosophers such as Epic-
tetus, Friedrich Nietzsche, and James Hillman. Amor fati
proposes that you take the whole of your life and love it
hard—the good, the bad, and the ugly.[1]

This concept marries well with James Hillman's "acorn
theory."[2] Acorn theory is an update on Aristotle's idea of
entelechy—the drive of all living things toward their true
form. Acorn theory holds "that each person bears a uniqueness that asks to be lived and that is already present before it
can be lived."[3] It is suffused with the spirit of amor fati in its
ardent embrace of the possibilities inherent in one's existence.

Within the acorn is encoded everything it needs to know to become the oak tree. It may not land in the best conditions, but that is out of the acorn's control, and such a circumstance does not diminish the acorn's true oak-ness. Even if it never gets the chance to fully become the oak tree, the acorn is Whole. The oakness of the acorn is inherent.

If we take amor fati (loving your life, the whole kit and caboodle) and marry it with acorn theory (this idea that all potentials of you are already present), we begin to approach the notion of Wholeness.

> *It's all there at once. When you look at a face before you, at a scene out your window or a painting on the wall, you see a whole gestalt. All the parts present themselves simultaneously. . . . It doesn't matter whether the painter put the reddish blotches in last or first, the gray streaks as afterthoughts. . . . What you see is exactly what you get, all at once. . . . So, too, the image in the acorn. You are born with a character; it is given; a gift, as the old stories say, from the guardians upon your birth.*
>
> —James Hillman

This remedy is an invitation to feel into the nature of your Wholeness and, as much as possible, wholly embrace yourself and your life as-is, where-is.

Anytime.

- Eight acorns (or if you can't find those, you can use eight dried kernels of corn, grain, or other seeds)
- Eight slips of paper
- A small vessel to hold the acorns in afterward

1. Write out each of the following statements, one on each slip of paper:

    The Whole abides in the present.

    The Whole embraces paradox and the rhythm of tension and yielding.

    The Whole is in touch with all parts of itself and every part belongs.

    The Whole cannot be known from any one perspective.

    The Whole can be sensed.

    The Whole thrives in mutual awareness and love.

    The Whole is emergent.

    The Whole is continuously renewing.

2. Create a large circle on the floor with the acorns positioned like the Wheel of the Year, stationed at the solstices, equinoxes, and halfway points in between. Under each acorn, place a slip of paper. With your

vessel in your hands, step into the center of the circle and ground yourself with a few settling breaths.

3. When you're ready, walk over to the first slip of paper you feel drawn to and pick it up along with the acorn. Read the written statement out loud. For a few moments, notice how the message feels in your body. Feel for the "oakness in the acorn." Then place the acorn and the paper in your vessel and move to the next station to the right.

4. Repeat this process at each station, saying each phrase aloud. How do these incantations feel in your body? Are there some that resonate more powerfully than others? Are there some that you wish you could embody more easily?

   What you experience may be implicit awareness that resists words. That's totally fine. Stay with that. Don't analyze or interpret it right now—that can come later in your journal. For now, continue simply to feel into Wholeness.

5. After you complete the round, stand or sit in the center of the circle. Imagine yourself as an acorn becoming an oak tree: your toes and legs rooting down deep into the soil, your torso strong and erect as the great

trunk, your arms long branches, your head and hair extending the canopy reaching skyward. All around you the little acorns begin to grow as well, your roots entwined.

Feel yourself as a part of the forest, then as a part of the Earth, along with all microbes of the soil and other subterranean kin, all the sea dwellers and sky travelers, all the beings with shoots and stalks and stems and trunks, all the two- and four-leggeds, and the ones who abide in the unseen realms. Be present with the Whole.

6. Read the slips of paper, this time replacing "The Whole" for the word "I":

    I abide in the present.

    I embrace paradox and the rhythm of tension and yielding.

    I am in touch with all parts of myself and every part belongs.

    I cannot be known from any one perspective.

    I can be sensed.

    I thrive in mutual awareness and love.

    I am emergent.

    I am continuously renewing.

7. To conclude, place your vessel on your altar or a windowsill for a full lunar cycle (another example of the ever-renewing Whole). During that time, practice

amor fati in your daily life.[4] Would your life feel different if you were to take as fact that your nature is Wholeness and every part belongs?

Author's Notes

1   "Amor Fati." Wikipedia. Accessed October 20, 2023. https://en.wikipedia.org/wiki/Amor_fati.

2   Hillman, James. *The Soul's Code: In Search of Character and Calling*, 1st ed. Random House, 1996.

3   This remedy is inspired by Philip Shepherd's work, in particular his thoughts on wholeness found in his book. Shepherd, Philip. *Radical Wholeness: The Embodied Present and the Ordinary Grace of Being.* North Atlantic Books, 2017.

    It is also inspired by the work of Octavia Butler, particularly: Butler, Octavia E. *Parable of the Sower.* Grand Central Publishing, 2023.

4   Even if it doesn't feel quite true and there remain parts of your life that you would reject (which would be totally understandable—philosophy and practical reality are often at odds!), nevertheless, proceed as though you regard yourself as Whole.

Acknowledgments

I'm so grateful to make my home on the lands of the Lekwungen-speaking peoples, the Songhees and the Esquimalt First Nations. The Spirits of Place here have supported my ritual practice since before I understood that's what was happening. Hay'sxw'qa! Thank you! My heart was planted and grew in this soil, and the love I feel, both for and from you, nourishes me and everyone my life touches.

Heartfelt thanks to my agent, Sharon Bowers, for believing in me. You make me feel like I have something to say and good enough words to say it. You're always gentle and kind and I appreciate you so much. Thanks also to the entire team at Countryman Press and W. W. Norton for championing my work.

I'm so lucky to have therapist, poet, and fellow author, Taraneh Erfan, as my first reader of this manuscript. Thank you for applying your sensitivity and keen intellect to my work, and helping me to be more thoughtful and brave.

I also want to acknowledge that as a white settler in spiritual leadership, my impact has not always been positive. I haven't always known what I now understand about white supremacy and how it interlocks with spirituality, capitalism, imperialism, heteronormativity, ableism, and patriarchy. The most foundational of these teachings, which resound in my intimate relationships on a daily basis, come from the work of the incomparable bell hooks and the experience of witnessing the Truth and Reconciliation Commission hearings in 2012. I appreciate the times I've been called out and called in, and I'm deeply grateful to teachers who've helped me integrate feedback on both a mental and spiritual level. Thank you to Desiree Adaway, Cyndi Brannen, and Dimitri de Morea. Special love to the friends in my antiracist caucus for all your wisdom, care, and ongoing accountability over the years: Jennie Biltek, Mara Cur, Megan Fredheim, and Jane Rioseco.

I'm indebted to the teachers who've instructed me on how to create a safe enough and solid enough ritual container. Some I've studied with formally, others I've observed and admired, and with a few I've been lucky enough to collaborate as colleagues and friends. Much respect and a thousand thank yous for a lifetime's worth of rich learning in this area: Thérèse Cator, Aftab Erfan, the late Hereditary Chief Leonard George, Tiffany Śwxeloselwet Joseph, Monique Gray Smith, Sparrow Hart, Shauna Janz, Sarah Kerr, Stephanie Papik, Norman Retasket, Madeleine Shaw, and Carolyne Taylor.

Authors and poets whose work has profoundly influenced my own and helped shape my thinking for this book include Steven Foster, Max Liboiron, Meredith Little, John O'Donohue, Joy Harjo, Mary Oliver, Jan Richardson, Malidoma Somé, Sobonfu Somé, Starhawk, and David Whyte. Thank you for your words and example.

I'm especially grateful to every student and fellow spiritual practitioner who has entered into ritual space with me. Thank you for your open hearts and sensitive souls. Thank you for your trust in me and in Spirit. Thank you for your magic.

Finally, thank you to my love, Ruben, for the Ritual of the Marriage Moon that ever renews our love and commitment. The mountain told me you'd come. The owl saved us from the brink. But it is you, flesh and bone, day in day out, who plunges hand into soil and pulls up stars to feed and nourish me, body, mind, and soul—it is you who both protects me and affirms my sovereignty. Thank you for being the safe and solid container I need to do my work.

Index

abusive relationships,
    183n1
Acknowledgment,
    Remedy for, 32,
    123–33
"acorn theory," 188–89
Aeolus, 18
aftercare, 6, 11
Agency, 4, 63, 64n2
Air, 14, 18–19, 74, 138
altered time, dissocia-
    tion and, 10
Alzheimer's, sugar
    and, 75
Ambiguous Loss, 93–95
ambivalence, 55
amor fati, 24, 188–89, 193
amulet, 42
Amun, 19
Anxiety, Ritual for, 32,
    41–47
Appreciation, Remedy
    of, 33, 134–39
appropriation, xixn3,
    35n7
Aristotle, 188
Arthur, Alua, 86, 91n9
Astromagic, 118n1,
    149n3, 183n4
attachment theory, 24,
    30, 37n18

attentive immobility, 8
Aura, 18
autistic burnout, 48
autoimmune disease,
    49
Awe, Remedy of, 32,
    140–45
Ayurveda, 14

Baez, Joan, 63
Balance, Remedy of, 32,
    146–50
Barbie, 143
"barefoot doctors," 3,
    33n1
bay, 101, 179
black women, 48–49,
    111
Body Mind Centering,
    169, 172n1
"brave space," 12, 34n3
British Psychological
    Society, 30
Burnout, Ritual of, 33,
    48–54
Butler, Octavia E.
    Cassandra and, 67
    Parable of the Sower,
    19–20, 36n10
    Wholeness Remedy
    and, 193n3

candles, 105n1
capitalization, 35n8
Cassandra, 65–67, 70n2
cedar, 128, 141
Celebration, Remedy
    of, 32, 151–55
change
    Octavia Butler on,
    19–20
    collapse skill, 169
    Fire and, 19
    Metal and, 21
    the Moon and, 116
    Rituals and, xvi, 12
    spell and, 14
    Truth and, 13
Chinese Five Element
    philosophy, 14
choice, 4
Coast Salish cultures,
    183n2
cocoon, 169, 172n3
collapse, ix–x, xviiin1
    change and, surren-
    dering to, 169
    collapse immobility, 8
    Elements and, 15
    freeze and, 13
    Metal and, 21
    the Numinous and,
    25

collapse (*continued*)
Remedies and, 27
"satisfiability" and, 36n17
Waning Crescent Moon and, 62
collective joy, 155n4
community, 6
Acknowledgment and, 125
appropriation and, 35
celebrations and, 155n3
Grief and, 87
Competent Protector, 79, 156–59
Confusion, Ritual of, 32, 55–59, 84
Connection, Remedy of, 32, 156–60
consent, 4
Conservation, Remedy of, 32, 33, 161–64
"contact nutrition," 159n1
containment, 7, 109
co-regulation, 7, 29, 134
Cosmic Egg, 26, 62
Cosmos
Acknowledgment Ritual and, 130
DNA and, 26
Numinous and, 25
Overwhelm Ritual and, 96
Cosmos: A Personal Voyage, 36n16
Creating a Nurture Surround, 172n2

"cultural artifact," 161–62, 164n2, 164n3
"cultural conservation," 161

"danced religion," 155n4
daydreaming, 10
Demodex mites, 16
denial, Disquiet and, 66
depersonalization stage, 49
derealization stage, 10, 49
Despair, Ritual of, 32, 60–64
dignity for all, 124
Dinner Party, The (Chicago), 70n3
dinosaurs, 22–23
Disquiet, Ritual of, 33, 65–70, 84n2
dissociation, 9, 10
DNA
Appreciation Remedy and, 138
Burnout Ritual and, 51
Dread Ritual and, 74
as an Element, 26–27
starstuff and, 36n16
"dose the field," 4, 12, 34n5
Dread, Ritual of, 32, 71–76
dreams, 13, 17
Dynamic Attachment Re-Patterning, 160n2
dysregulation, 29, 49

Earth
Appreciation Remedy and, 136
Awe Remedy and 144
Dread Ritual and, 74
as an Element, 14–16
love and, 27
plastic and, 23
Sun-and-Earth goddess, 60
effectiveness, 13
Elements, 13–27
Air, 18–19
DNA, 26–27
Earth, 15–16
Fire, 19–20
Metal, 21–22
Numinous, 24–26
Plastic, 22–24
Water, 17
Embodied Presence Process, The (TEPP), 149n1
endorphins, 112, 151
enoughness, 28, 142
entelechy, 188
Erfan, Taraneh, 33n2, 91n9, 195–96
expressive writing, 41–47

Fall, activities and, 32
Fear, Ritual of, 32, 77–84
feasting, 155n4
Feng Popo, 18
feng shui, 14, 183n2
fennel, 179
fetish, 42

fir, 128
Fire, 14, 19–21, 74, 138
Ford, Christine Blasey, 67
Freeze, x, xviiin2
   collapse and, x, 13
   coming out of, 8–11
   confusion and, 55
   mobilization and, 9–11
   positive aspect of, 9
   remedies and, 27
   ritual and, 7
   types of, 8
Friday, 118n1, 157
functional freeze, 8

Goddess in the Hole, 61
Good Grief Network, 86
gratitude, 134–35
Greater Good Science Center, 64n2, 140, 145n1
Grief
   Confusion Ritual and, 57
   Ritual of, 85–92
   safeness and, 11
   Winter and, 33
Grief Vigil, 87, 88, 90
grounding, 4, 15, 146
gut flora, 16

H.A.L.T., 6
"healing hangover," 5
Hekate, 60, 183
Heller, Diane Poole
   attachment theory and, 37n18

"contact nutrition," 159n1
"dose the field," 34n5
Dynamic Attachment Re-Patterning, 160n2
Hestia, 20
Heumann, Judy, 67
Hill, Anita, 67
Hillman, James, 188–89
Hittites, 60
house elf, 183n2
house poles, 183n2
humility, 5
Huracan, 19

Indigenous peoples, 22–23, 124, 138n2, 155n4
inspiration, 64n2
"it's giving," 174, 177n1

Janz, Shauna, 85–86, 91n6
Juniper, 101, 128, 179
Jupiter, 118n1

Land
   Competent Protectors and, 79
   Conservation Remedy and, 161
   Indigenous concepts of, 22–23
   Land Acknowledgment, 124
land, humility and, 5
Le Guin, Ursula, 67
Liboiron, Max, xixn3, 22, 35n8

Listener, 127–30, 132n3
Little Lifts, 151, 154n2
Loa Bade, 19
Long Emergency, 3
Lorde, Audre, 108, 113n2
Loss, Ritual of, 32, 93–95
love spell, 156–60
lunar day, 146, 149n2
lung, 173n5

Madame Wind, 18
Mars, 118n1
memory loss, dissociation and, 10
Mercury, 116, 118n1
Metal, 14, 21–22, 74, 138
Meyers, Nancy, xiii
Michael, 151–52
Mingus, Mia, 67
mobilization, 9–11
Monday, 115–16, 118n1, 181
Moon
   Balance remedy and, 146–49
   Confusion Ritual and, 56
   Despair Ritual and, 61–62
   Fear Ritual and, 78
   Grief Ritual and, 88
   lunar day, 149n2
   Mondays and, 118n1
   personalities and, 61–62
   planetary magic and, 116, 118n1

Moon (*continued*)
  Protection remedy, 181
  remedy chapters and, 32
  Renewal remedy, 185
  ritual chapters and, 31–32
  Ritual of the Marriage Moon, xiv–xvi, 197
  Water Element and, 17
Movement, Remedy of, 32, 165–68
movement, Satisfaction Cycle and, 169
mugwort, 101, 179
mutual self-help, 6
Mysterium tremendum et fascinans, 24

narcissism, 126, 131n2
Natural Step Framework, 164n2
nature, 35n8
nettle, 101, 183n2
NeuroAffective Relational Model (NARM), 172n2
NeuroAffective Touch Therapy, 172n2
neurobiology, 6, 30
New Age Movement, 36n16
Nietzsche, Friedrich, 188
Numinous, as an Element, 24–26, 74, 138

Numinous Podcast, The, xviii, 91n6, 119, 149n3, 154n1, 183n4
Numinous Quest, 77
Nurturance
  Confusion Ritual and, 57
  Remedy of, 33, 169–73
  Water and, 17

One Billion Rising campaign, 155n4
Orphic Hymns, 183n4
Otto, Rudolf, 24
oversoul, 35n8
Overwhelm, Ritual of, 11, 96–101

Parable of the Sower (Butler), 19–20, 36n10, 193n3
parasympathetic nervous system, 76n4
pendulation, 29
pepper, 179
perfectionism, healing from, 164n3
personal mythwork, 37n18
phytoplankton, 22
Picatrix, 147, 149n3
pine, 128
planetary magic, 116
plants
  Appreciation Remedy and, 134–39
  Competent Protectors and, 79

Earth element and, 15
the home and, 183
kin, nonhuman and, 92n10
levels, 101
Loss and, 95n5
Overwhelm Ritual and, 96–101
plant connection, 138n2
Plastic and, 22
protective, 179
Plastic, as an Element, 22–24, 74, 138
plastic, Max Liboiron on, xixn3
Pleasure Activism (brown), 36n17
poignance, 24
Politics of Trauma, The (Haines), 36n17
Pollution Is Colonialism (Liboiron), 22, xixn3, 35n8
polyvagal theory, 30, 37n18
potlatches, 155n4
Power Threat Meaning framework, 30–31
Predicament, Ritual of, 32, 102–6
prefrontal cortex, 127, 133
Pronking, Remedy of, 32, 174–77
protection, evergreen boughs and, 128
Protection, Remedy of, 33, 178–84

Proust questionnaire, 151

psychic numbness, 10

PTMF, 30–31

Pyne, Stephen J., 20

"pyrocene," 20

Quaker elder, 151

Rage, Ritual for, 32, 108–13

Rage Role Models, 109, 111

Remedies, xvii–xviii
  Agency, 63
  the Moon and, 32
  as resources, 27–29
  safeness and, 11
  self-care and, 6
  storylines and, 31
  World-Building, 63

Renewal, Remedy of, 32, 185–87

residential schools, 123, 131n1

resilience
  Acknowledgment and, 129–30
  Burnout and, 49
  Celebration and, 154
  Remedies and, 27
  Renewal remedy and, 185
  "satisfiability"

resourcing, 29

ritual, xvi, 7
  containment and, 7, 12
  days of the week and, 118n1

ecofeminist witch-craft and, 37n18

Elements of, 13–27

mobilization and, 9–11

the Moon and, 31–32

safeness and, 11

seasons and, 32, 37n18, 37n20

storylines and, 31

transformation and, 11

Ritual of the Marriage Moon, xiv, 197

rosehip, 179

rosemary, xv, 101, 179, 183n2

safeness, 11–13
  abusive relationships and, 183n1
  Appreciation remedy and, 134
  Awe and, 141
  diaphragmatic breathing and, 47
  orienting to, 180, 183n1
  Rage Ritual and, 109
  Resourcing and, 29
  rituals and remedies and, xvii, 4, 11, 12, 77
  trauma response and, 34n4

"safe place," 11

Satisfaction Cycle, 169

"satisfiability," 28, 36n17

Saturday, 118n1, 181

Saturn, 118n1, 181

Schapira, Laurie Layton, 66

seasons, 32–33, 37n18

seeds, 185–87, 190

self-regulation, 29, 132n4

Shepherd, Philip, 149, 193n3

sigils, 105

sleep disturbances, 172n3

slow, 5

Smith, Monique Gray, 168

somatics, 29, 34n5, 36n17, 172n1

Sparrow Hart, 59n2, 84n1

spells, definition of, xvi–xvii, 7, 14, 16

Spirits of Place, 5

spiritual power tools, 42

Spoon Theory, 106n4

Spring, activities and, 32

spruce, 128

Stagnation, Ritual of, 32, 114–19

starstuff, 27, 36n16

Sufis, 155n4

sugar, Alzheimer's and, 75n2

Summer, activities and, 32

Sun, the
  Appreciation Remedy and, 136
  Numinous Podcast and, 118n1, 149n3
  Renewal Remedy and, 185–86
  Sunday and, 118n1

Sun-and-Earth goddess, 60
Sunday, the Sun and, 118n1
support, 6
sympathetic nervous system, 76n4, 119n2

talisman, 42
TEPP, 149n1
therapeutic journaling, 41, 47n1
therapy, the political and, 37n18. *See also* therapies by name
Thor, 18
Thursday, Jupiter and, 118n1
thyme, 101, 179
titration, 29
tonic immobility, 8
transcendence, 25–26
transparency, 5
trauma
    bedrooms and, 173n4
    containment and release and, 7
    freeze and, 11
    healing and, xi–xii
    Diane Poole Heller and, 160n2
    NARM and, 172n2
    safeness and, 11–12, 34n4

satisfiability and, 36n17
turbulent times and, 108
witchcraft and, 3–6, 12, 33n2, 132
tree magic, 128
Truth, 13, 124
Truth and Reconciliation Commission (TRC), 123, 124, 131n1, 196
Truth Wheel, 56–58
Tuesday, Mars and, 118n1
Tuqan, Fadwa, 92n9, 110

ventral vagus, 159
Venus, 118n1, 157, 183n4
Vesta, 20
Vigil, 85–92

Water, 14, 17
    Acknowledgment and, 131
    Appreciation and, 136–38
    Balance and, 146–49
    Burnout and, 50–53
    Dread and, 73–76
    Nurturance and, 170–71
    Overwhelm, 97–101

Renewal and, 186–87
    vigil and, 90
Wednesday, Mercury and, 116, 118n1
Western occult traditions, 14
white supremacy culture, 164n3
Wholeness, Remedy of, 188–93
Wiccan religion, 14
"Wild Geese" (Oliver), 168n4
Winter, activities and, 33
witch archetype, 37n18
witchcraft
    ecofeminist, 37n18
    trauma-informed, 3–6, 33n2
    trauma-sensitive, 12, 132n3
witnessing, 6, 77, 126, 196
Woman, Life, Freedom movement, 155n4
Wong, Alice, 67, 110
World-Building, 63–64
"World egg," 36n15
wuxing tradition, 14

Yes, And!, 166, 167n2

zooplankton, 22

About the Author

Carmen Spagnola teaches about animism, folk magic, witchcraft, ritual, and ancestral knowledge related to land and seasons. She cross-pollinates somatics, attachment, collapse awareness, intersectional feminism, and kinship with the More Than Human in her work as a trauma resolution practitioner. Carmen is the author of *The Spirited Kitchen: Recipes and Rituals for the Wheel of the Year,* which teaches folklore and spellcraft for the solstices, equinoxes, and halfway points between, based on her training in culinary arts at Le Cordon Bleu Paris and many years catering her Wheel of the Year workshops.

Carmen's professional study includes extensive training in hypnotherapy, interpersonal neurobiology, somatic psychology, mood and personality disorder support, and client-centered assistance for neurodivergent adults, youth, and their caregivers. She is constantly researching current promising practices to provide psychoemotional care and nervous system reconditioning support for people with chronic or episodic disability, with special attention to autoimmunity, dysautonomia, and long COVID. She holds provider certifications for Dynamic Attachment Re-Patterning, The Safe and Sound Protocol, Tension and Trauma Releasing Exercises, The Resilience Toolkit, and Clinical Hypnotherapy. Her spiritual healing repertoire includes numerous certificates spanning a twenty-five-year exploration of trancework, regression therapy, energy work, shamanistic practices, systemic constellations, divination, herbalism, kitchen witchery, cultural conservation and ancestral veneration practices, and wilderness quest.

An outspoken socialist feminist witch, Carmen has been teaching, speaking, and writing about anticolonial, antiracist, anticapitalist, antioppression, and class-conscious themes as necessary components of spiritual healing for over a decade. The Truth and Reconciliation Commission of Canada's 94 Calls to Action deeply inform her life and she continues to study methods of collective healing to address trans-generational trauma caused by whiteness. Her philosophy is unreservedly shared on her show, *The Numinous Podcast,* and practiced in her online community, The Numinous Network.

Carmen's special ancestral kinships include Horse, Dog, Deer, Salmon, Nettle, Rose, and Mountain.

For supplemental audio recordings of selected rituals and remedies found in this book, visit carmenspagnola.com/spellsfortheapocalypse.